AF262602

Designing Dynamism

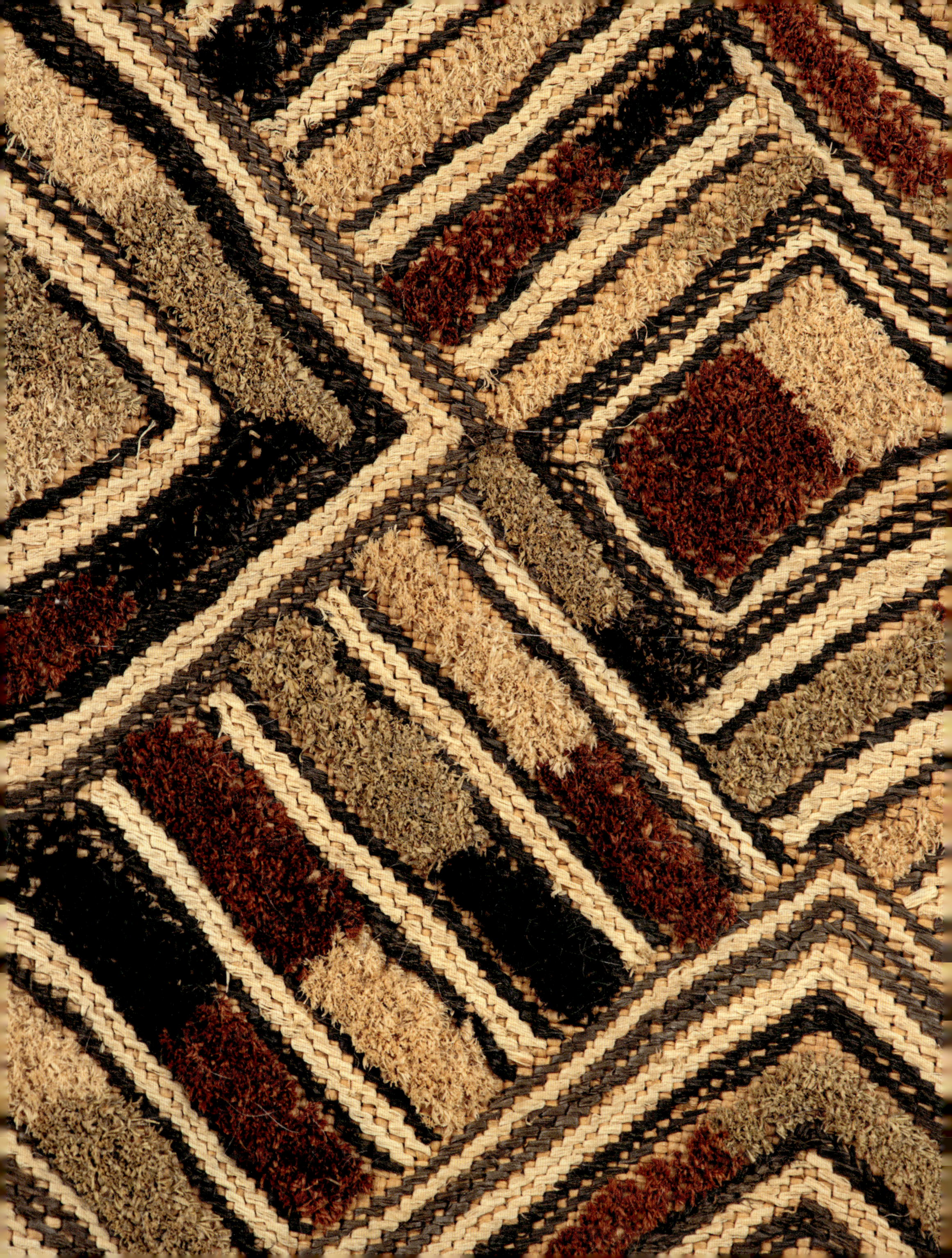

Designing Dynamism

Kuba Textiles from the D R Congo,
The Wesley Mancini Collection

Annie Carlano, **editor**
Vanessa Drake Moraga
Malika Leiper
Stephen Burks
Todd A. Herman

Illustrations by Joel Smeltzer

The Mint Museum
in association with D Giles Limited

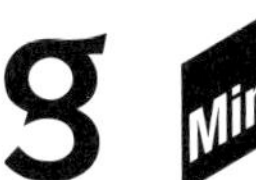

Contents

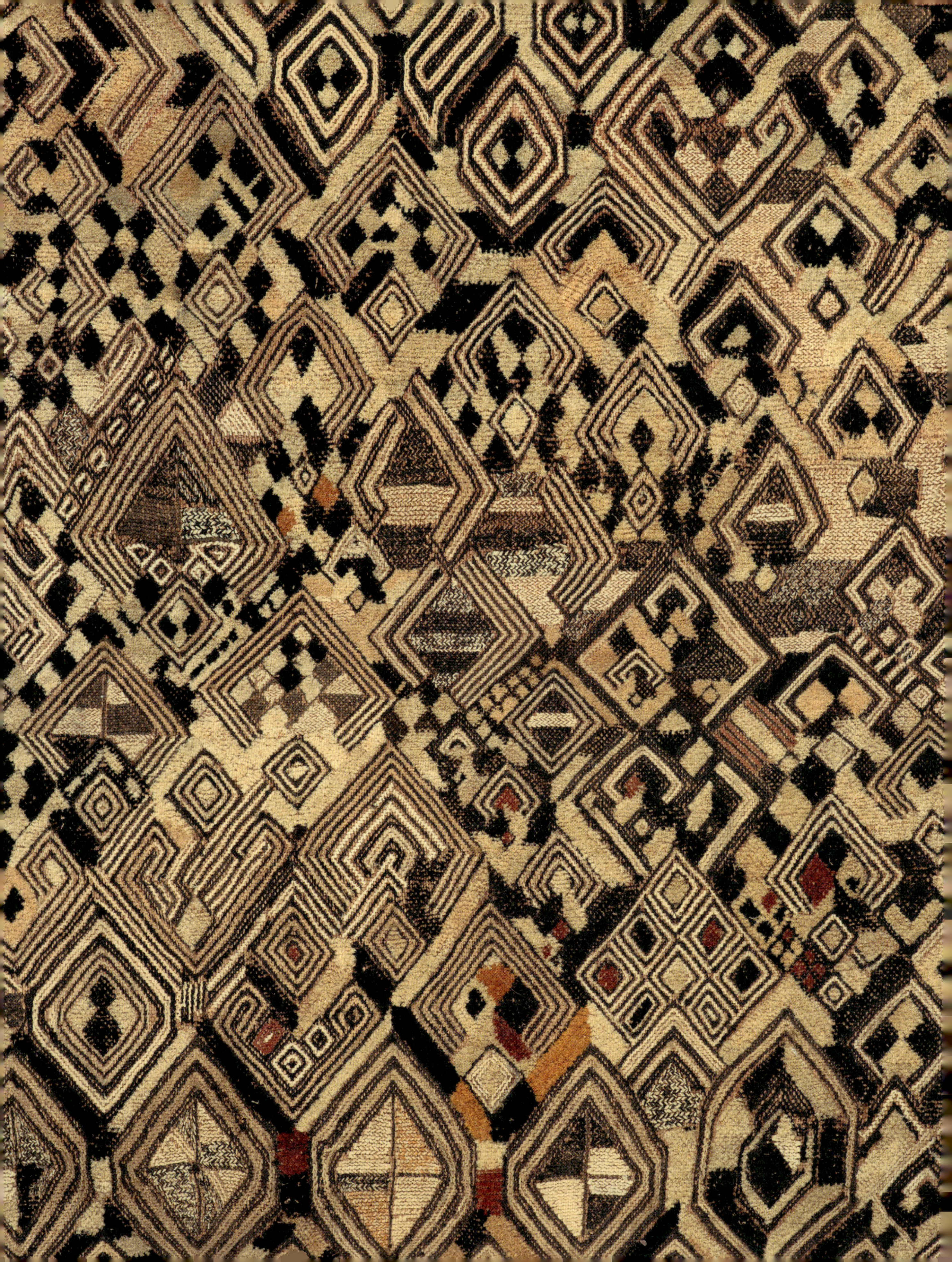

Foreword

Annie Carlano
Senior Curator, Craft, Design & Fashion, The Mint Museum

Todd A. Herman, PhD
President & CEO, The Mint Museum

Collectors from throughout the United States and abroad have gifted single objects and entire collections to the Mint Museum. Over the past decade, substantial holdings of craft and design have entered our collection due to the generosity of those closer to home, from the Porter • Price donation of jewelry by Robert Ebendorf and his students, to Lorne Lassiter and Gary Ferraro's gift of Japanese and Western objects. This book and coinciding exhibition celebrate the recent gift of over fifty prestige textiles by the Kuba people (Shoowa group) from Wesley Mancini, a Charlotte-based textile designer and longtime friend of the museum. Mancini, who saw his first Kuba textile while a graduate student at Cranbrook Academy of Art, has a deep knowledge of textile history, weaving and embroidery techniques, and patterning that led him to marvel at the distinctive syncopation of Kuba prestige cloth designs, and eventually to build a collection that captures their dazzling range of non-repeating motifs.

From the remote Kasai region of what is now south-central Democratic Republic of Congo, several Kuba subgroups created appliqué and embroidered textiles for their kings' regalia, dance costumes, everyday dress and utilitarian furnishings, and as gifts or funerary offerings to a king or a dignitary. The prestige panels that Mancini collected may have been made for Kuba use, or for export, or some of each;

regardless, the patterns and the craftsmanship are superb. These textiles are the focus of the exhibition, *Designing Dynamism: Kuba Textiles from the D R Congo, The Wesley Mancini Collection*.

Living with Kuba textiles on the walls of his home and company office (protected from light, of course, and archivally framed!), Wesley Mancini drew inspiration from them for several of his own jacquard weavings. Four of his recent textile designs were also gifted to the Mint and are included in *Designing Dynamism*.

The Mint Museum is known for its collections of modern and contemporary art and design and strives to integrate them into a more comprehensive understanding of the zeitgeist of a given era. Kuba textiles have interested artists and designers in the West for over a hundred years, and particularly in the early twentieth century. But while the impact of African sculpture on modernism has been well documented, the extent to which textiles—and Kuba textiles, specifically—were admired, collected, and influential on artists is less known. Vanessa Drake Moraga's years of research on the topic are captured brilliantly in the lead essay of this catalogue. Providing a counterpoint to her text, Stephen Burks reminds us that, despite colonialism and corruption (both political and aesthetic), the craft of Kuba textiles remains a living tradition with a vibrant future. Dan Giles and his

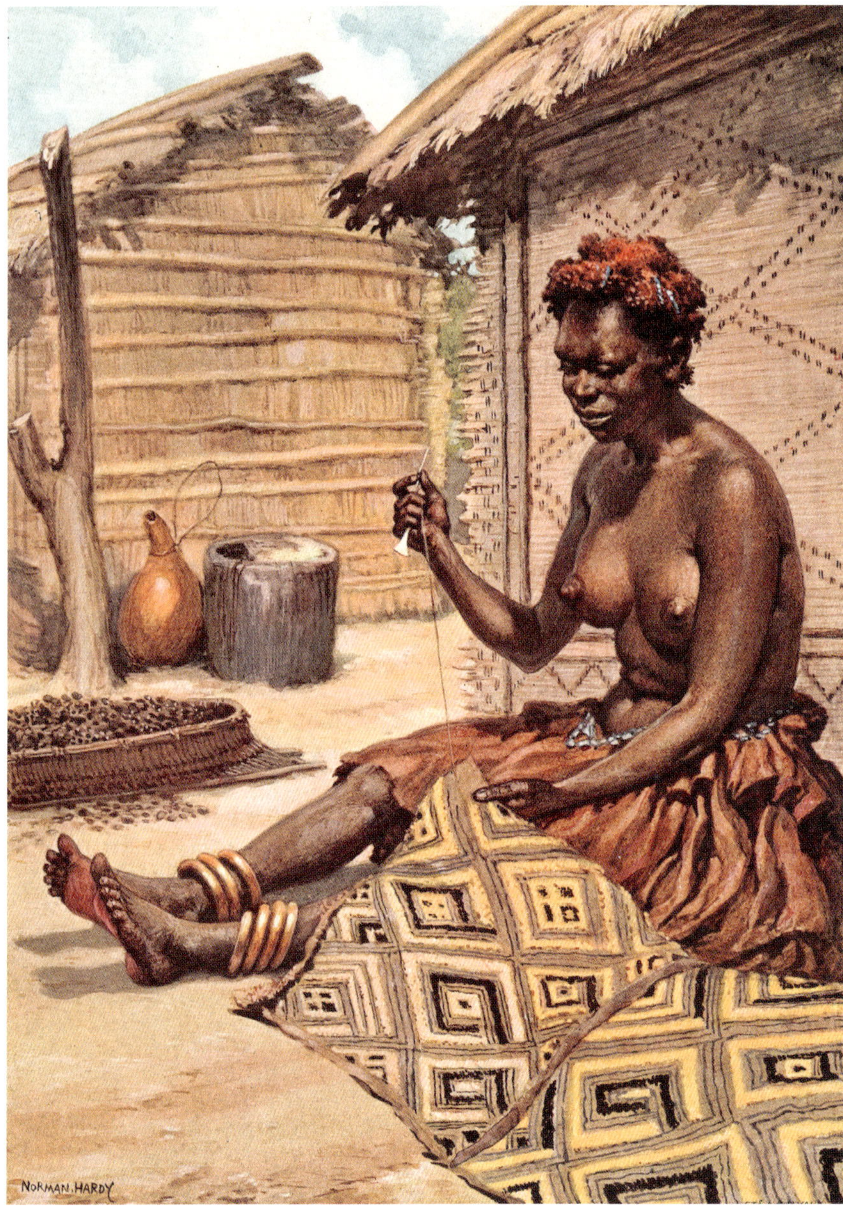

Cat. 3 (left)
Norman H. Hardy (British, 1864–1914), Bangongo embroiderer, from Torday and Joyce, *Notes ethnographiques sur les peuples communément appelés Bakuba* (1910), plate VIII
Schomburg Center for Research in Black Culture, Jean Blackwell Hutson. Research and Reference Division, The New York Public Library

Cat. 4 (right)
Eliot Elisofon (American, 1911–1973), Kuba man at his loom, Nemwele village, Congo (Democratic Republic), 1970.
EEPA EECL 7181, Eliot Elisofon Photographic Archives, National Museum of African Art, Smithsonian Institution

team at D Giles Limited have designed a book that echoes the dynamic geometry and textures of the prestige panels.

Creating an innovative setting for *Designing Dynamism* has been a monumental undertaking. Stephen Burks and Malika Leiper's exhibition design supports the narrative with sensitivity and joy, highlighting the beautifully conserved and mounted textiles, prepared by conservator Howard Sutcliffe. As always, it is the members of the Mint staff who make the magic happen. Dr. Herman thanks Annie Carlano, curator of the exhibition and Senior Curator of Craft, Design & Fashion, for her vision and for assembling such top talent; they both acknowledge the entire Collections & Exhibitions team for such excellent work.

Jay Everette and Wells Fargo have our immense gratitude for once again going above and beyond to make *Designing Dynamism: Kuba Textiles from the D R Congo, The Wesley Mancini Collection* an outstanding contribution to art history.

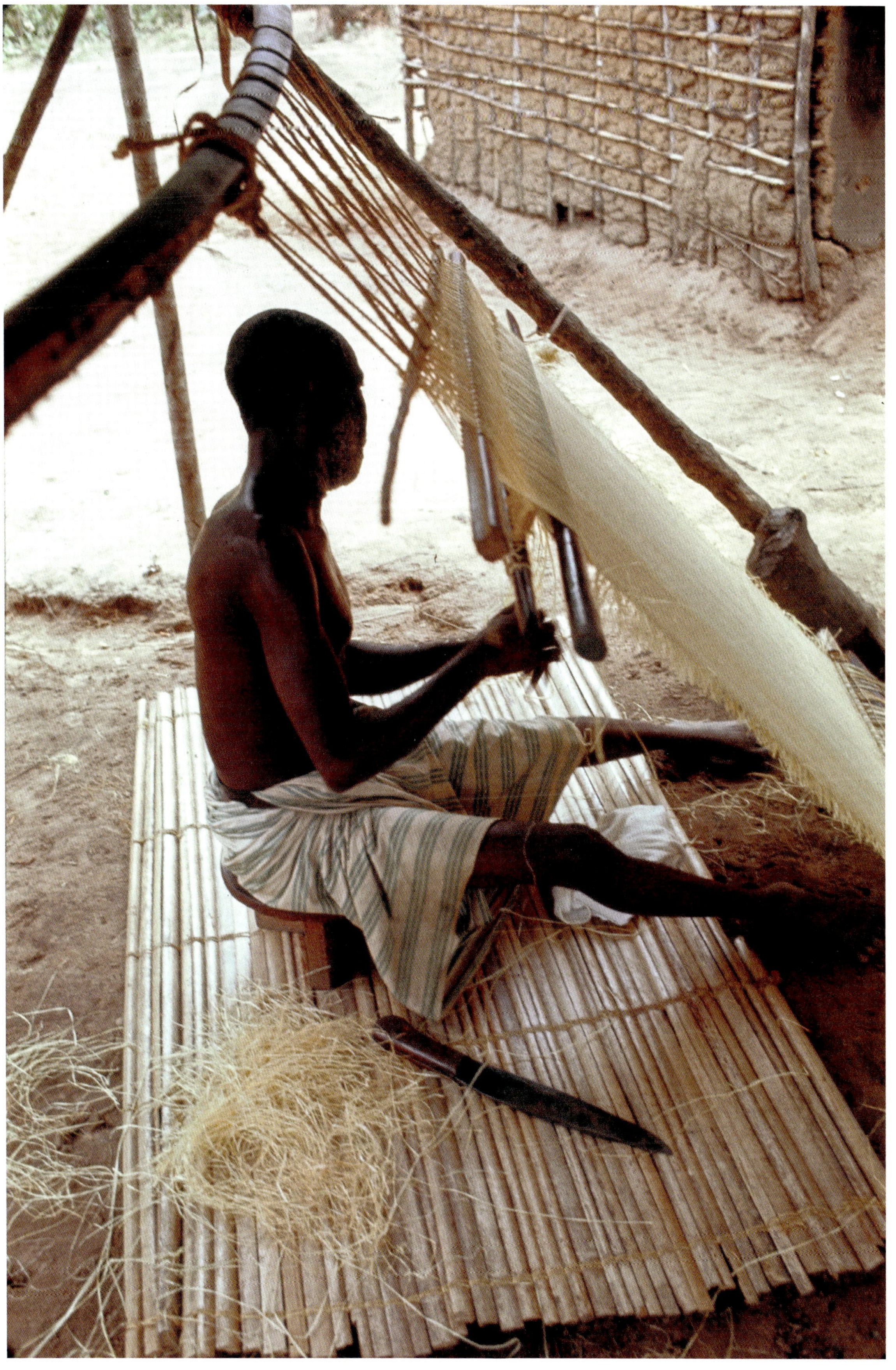

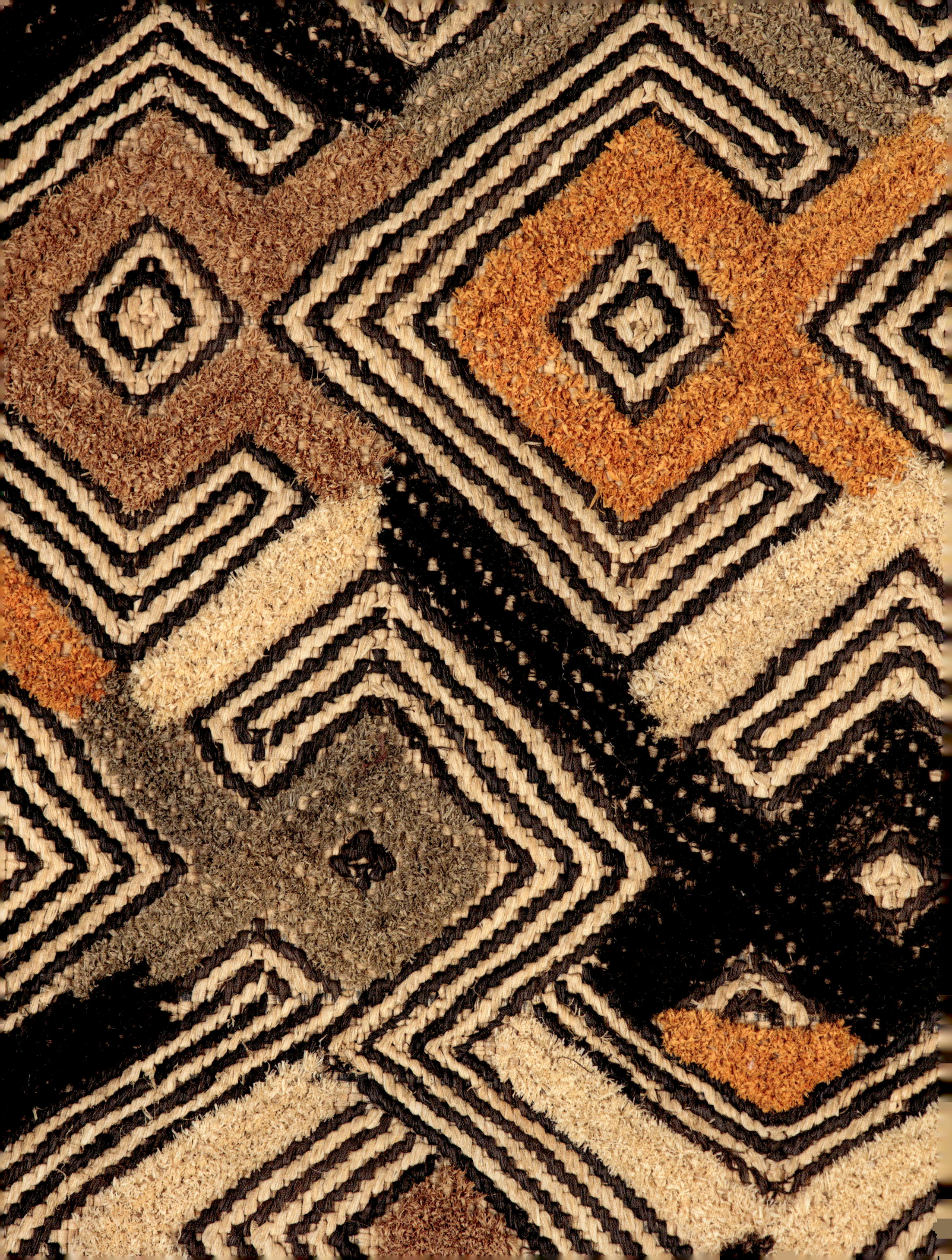

Sponsor's Statement

Design is all around us and impacts every aspect of our lives. Everything—
from what we live in, travel in, dress in, to the devices we hold in our hands
or type on—was conceived by someone or a team to solve a problem and
enhance our lives: how to achieve better functionality, how to communicate
an idea, how to express identity and culture. When it comes to textiles,
pattern, texture, and color carry the message. We admire the abstraction of
modern weavings of the Diné and the Bauhaus, Amish quilts and the quilts
of Gee's Bend. With regard to African textiles, the Kente cloth of the Asante/
Ashanti people of Ghana is well known but we are less aware of the other
extraordinary fabrics from pan-African countries, especially the unique
instinctive geometry of Kuba textiles.

*Designing Dynamism: Kuba Textiles from the D R Congo, The Wesley
Mancini Collection* brings our attention to the powerful patterns and
rich textures of Kuba prestige cloth, its history and impact. Wells Fargo
is pleased to be the presenting sponsor of this book and exhibition, and
supports the Mint Museum's intent to tell the story of design history and
illuminate the skill and craft of its makers.

Jay Everette
National Director of Community Relations
Philanthropy and Community Impact
Wells Fargo Public Affairs

Cat. 5
Prestige Panel (detail),
27⅛ × 25⅝ × 1¼ inches
(68.9 × 65.1 × 3.2 cm) (framed).
2020.24.25

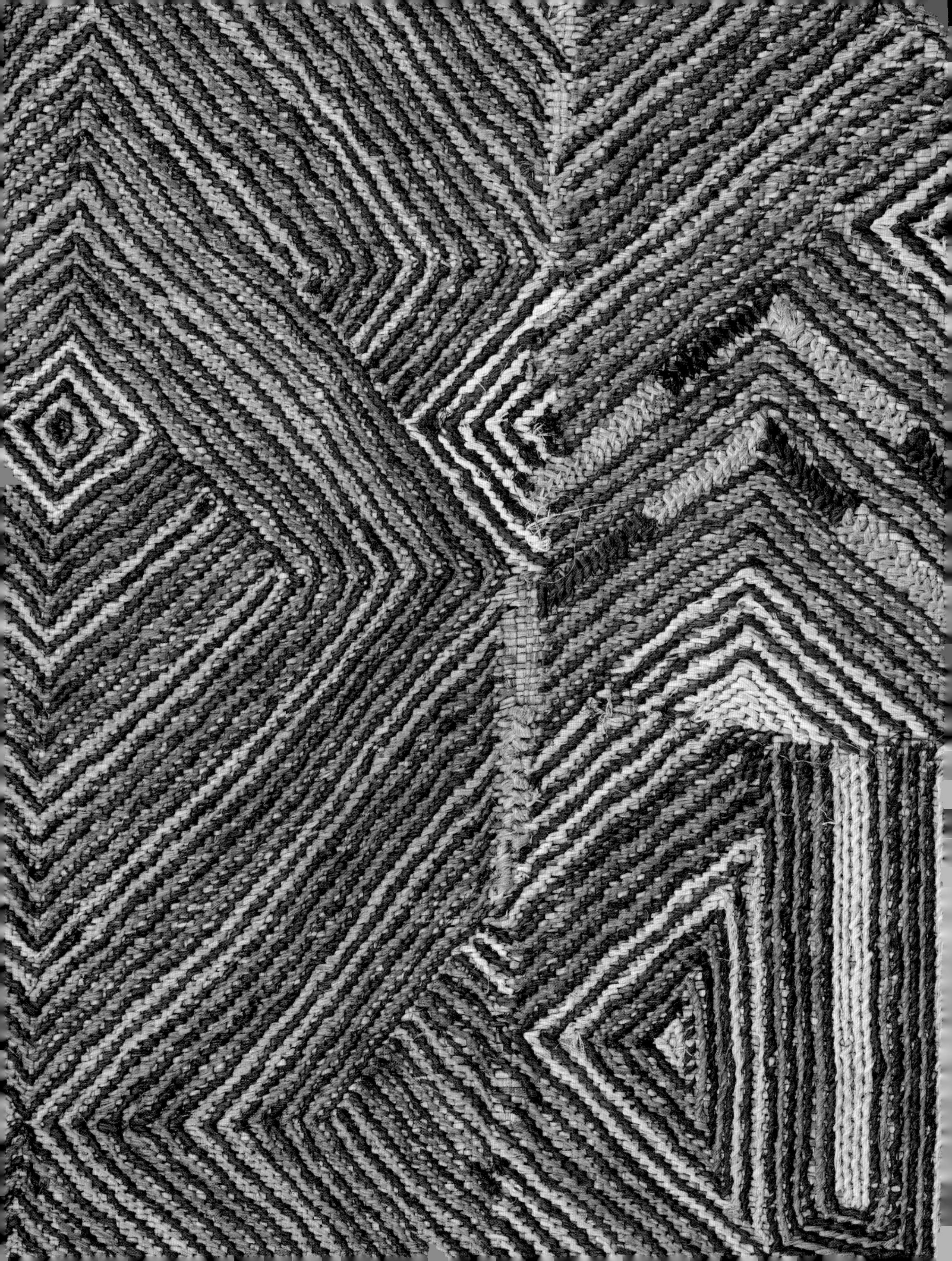

Designing Dynamism
The Past, Present, and Future of Kuba Textiles

Stephen Burks and Malika Leiper

"In order for any craft to have a future, it must have a present."

I had seen Kuba textiles in photographs before, but never in person until I visited Charlotte, North Carolina. On a humid September afternoon at the Mint Museum, I was led between dimly lit corridors of shelving racks from which blue-gloved hands unpacked one Kuba cloth after another, and placed them before me to behold in wonder. My eyes searched for patterns, a moment of consistency or repetition, and failed. From a distance, the dense raffia threads depicted a timeless organic geometry—a visual force like no other. But, up close, an entirely new landscape of cut-pile fibers emerged. In each strand of the material, I sensed the creative intelligence of the hands that made it. No one cloth was like the next—each piece was a living work of art. A primary form. Original and essential.

From the moment of their so-called "discovery" by European missionaries and explorers in the nineteenth century, the iconic motifs of the Kuba people have continued to transfix their viewers. No doubt, many, including myself, could not resist the temptation to attempt to decode the messages hidden in their design, the way modern masters like Henri Matisse would sit, "waiting for something to come from the mystery of their instinctive geometry."[1] But one need only recall the 1923 exhibition at the Brooklyn Museum, whose title—"Primitive Negro Art, Chiefly From the Belgian Congo"—illuminates the problematic enterprise of cultural exchange emanating from the unchallenged centrality of the West.[2] As a result of this very process, the material output of the Kuba people remains largely confined to museums in Europe and America, where it is preserved as artifacts of a bygone civilization; or in the tribal art markets in

Cat. 6
Prestige Panel (detail),
19¾ × 19⅜ inches
(50.2 × 49.2 cm).
2020.24.39

Amsterdam and Brussels alongside so-called "primitive" African statuary, where their aesthetic appeal as "ethnic" is further codified and marketed to contemporary consumers.

How, then, to imagine a future for Kuba textiles if generations of cultural, material, and intellectual extraction have rendered it a dead or lost art form? In order for any craft to have a future, it must have a present. Today, the Democratic Republic of the Congo—where the Kuba civilization once thrived—is a population of young people under the age of thirty. Much like the rest of the continent, it is a country with a deep history complicated by destructive European influence and an assumed truncated future cut short by limited scholarly imagination.[3] Meanwhile, according to the United Nations, more than half of global population growth between now and 2050 is expected to occur in Sub-Saharan Africa.

Naming this exhibition "Designing Dynamism" acknowledges the creative capacity of the descendants of the Kuba civilization, as well as the transformative potential of design. The more we recognize that the future will be created by all of us, including those in the parts of the globe where the majority of the world resides,[4] the more craft traditions, like Kuba, can evolve and continue to serve the needs of society. After all, what is the distinguishing factor between "luxury" and "craft", other than a relational superiority predisposed towards the West? Let us take this present moment, as we honor the mastery of Kuba textile arts, as an invitation to re-invest in their future and the people that make them. By doing so, we may finally see that, much like the graphic language of the cloth itself, the future of Kuba is very much alive, ever-changing, and moving dynamically within the present.

Cat. 7 (opposite)
Norman H. Hardy (British, 1864–1914), Kwete Peshanga Kena in ceremonial dress, from Torday and Joyce, *Notes ethnographiques sur les peuples communément appelés Bakuba* (1910), plate II
Schomburg Center for Research in Black Culture, Jean Blackwell Hutson. Research and Reference Division, The New York Public Library

Cat. 8 (following spread)
Prestige Panel (detail), 24⅞ × 24½ × 1¼ inches (63.2 × 62.2 × 3.2 cm) (framed). 2020.24.17

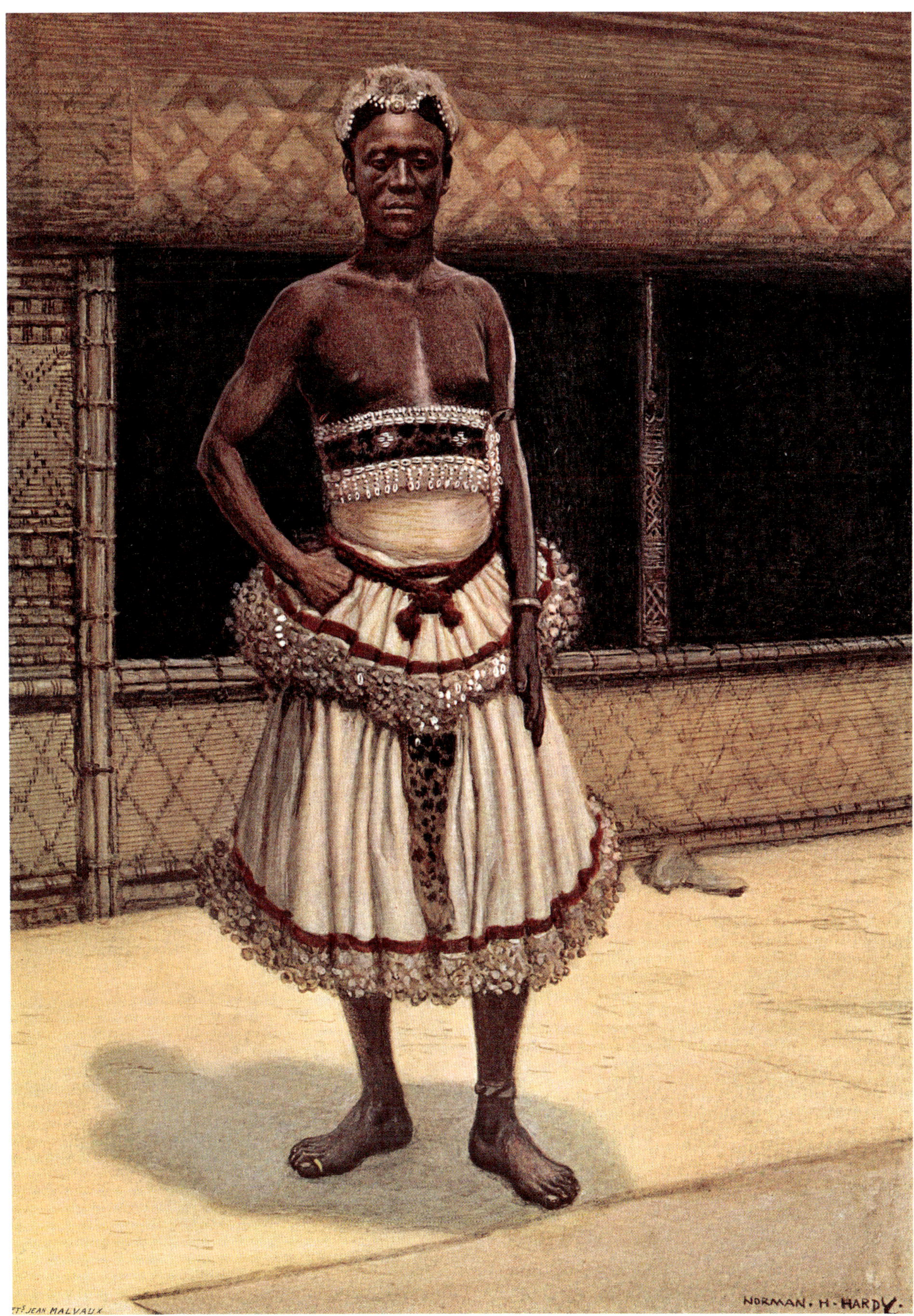

ᵗˢ JEAN MALVAUX
NORMAN·H·HARDY·

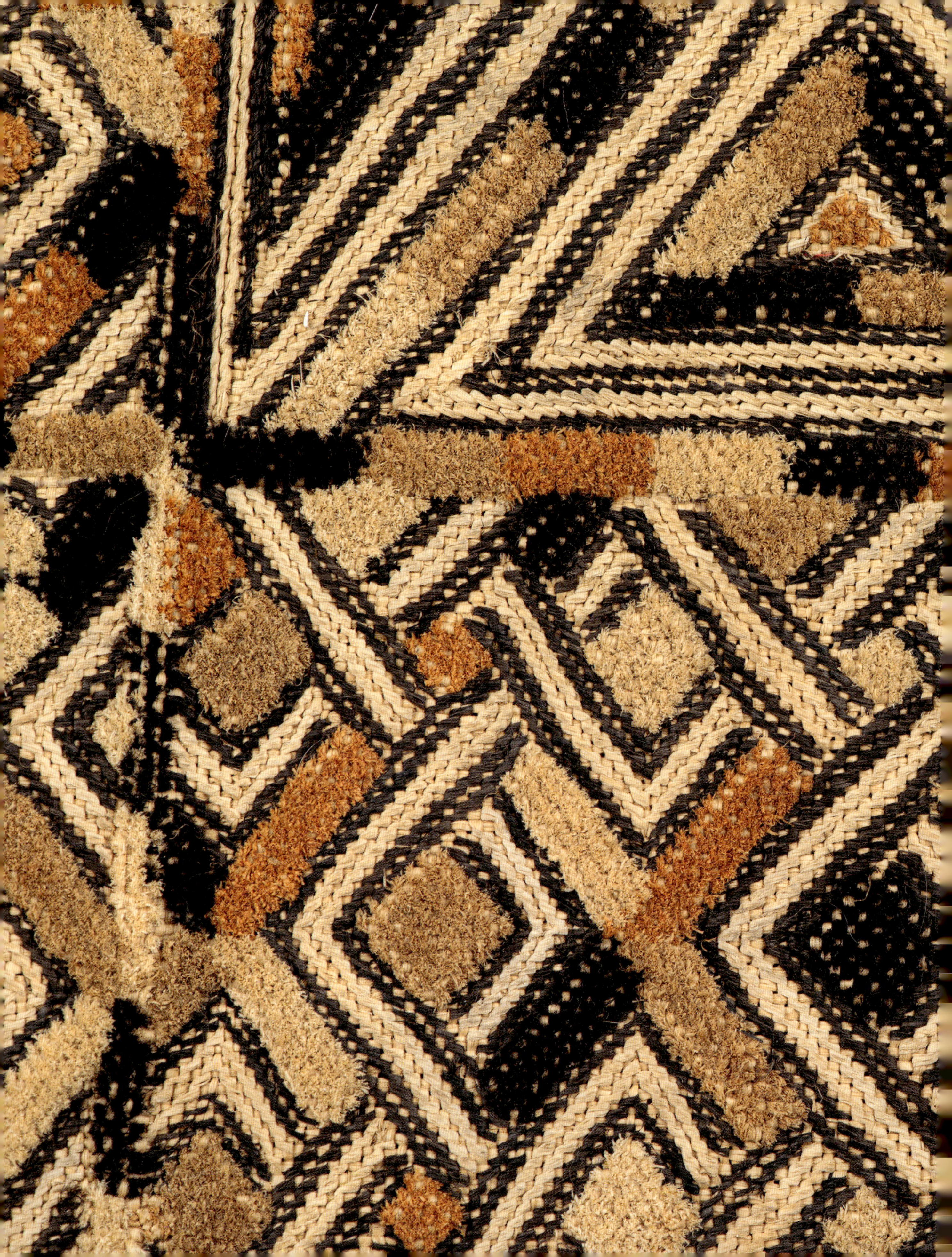

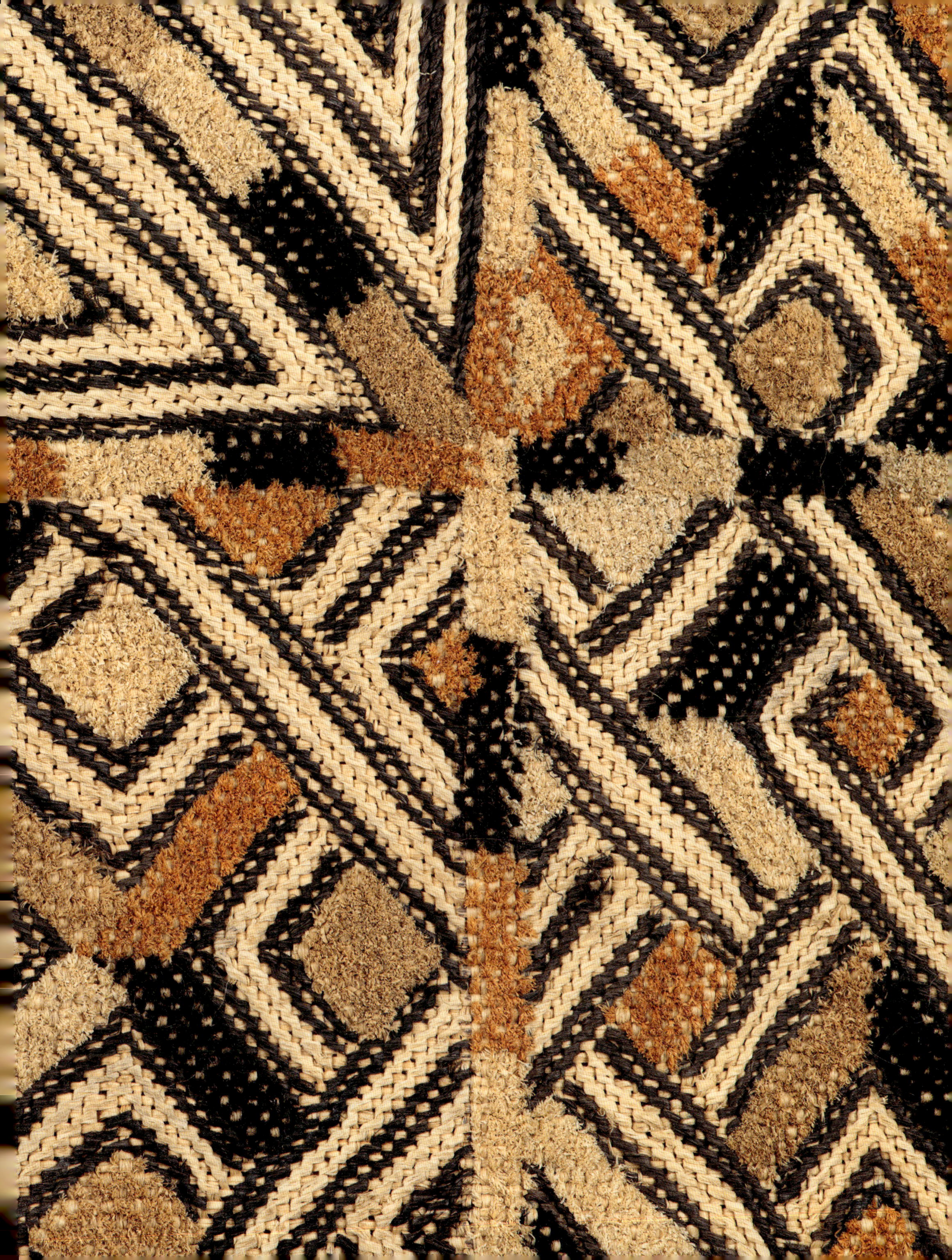

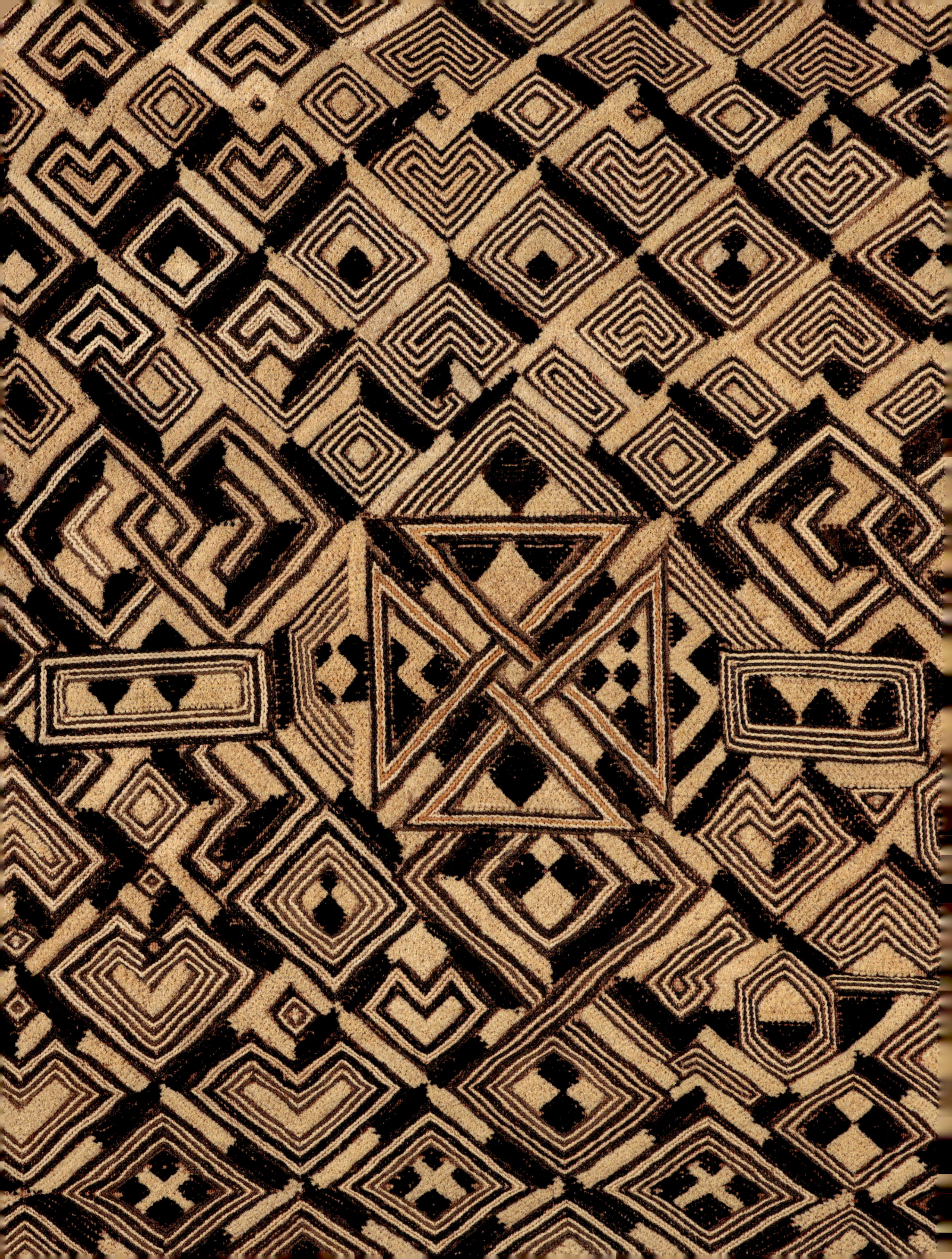

Patterns of Influence
Kuba Textile Art as Inspiration in Twentieth-Century Design

Vanessa Drake Moraga

Origins

Textiles from the Congo—fine raffia cloths of golden hues embellished with textural geometric patterning—first arrived in Europe between the sixteenth and seventeenth centuries. Among the highly acclaimed diplomatic gifts and trade goods shipped from the powerful Kongo kingdoms to the courts and ethnology collections of European aristocrats were woven raffia cushions trimmed with pompoms and tassels, reminiscent of the luxurious piled and silken versions used in Europe. These rare objects almost certainly represent the earliest examples of a Central African textile adapted to a European format.[5]

The coastal Kongo kingdoms in the vicinity of the lower Congo River were decimated by five centuries of European colonization and the devastating repercussions of slavery and the expropriation of the wealth of natural resources that came in its wake. Far into the interior of the present-day Democratic Republic of the Congo, however, a comparable great royal federation with an ancient history continued to flourish. In the multi-ethnic Kuba kingdom, an indigenous textile culture of extraordinary artistic and technical accomplishment remained intact and creatively vital through the twentieth century.

The plush Kongo weavings were likened to velvets and satins by the chroniclers of the time. Some three hundred years later, their descriptions were echoed in the epithet "Kasai velvets" that was given to a related type of prestige or status cloth obtained by Western colonialists navigating the Sankuru and Kasai rivers in the 1880s–1890s. The rivers marked the northern and western boundaries of the kingdom, which encompassed at least nineteen groups (including Bushong and Shoowa), each making a subtly different contribution to the multifaceted Kuba design aesthetic.

In the Kuba tradition, as in Kongo weaving, the size of the square or rectangular woven panels reflected the typical length of processed raffia palm fiber filaments that could not be spun into longer threads (about 25 inches, or 65 cm). This inspired a modular style of textile fabrication with garments, such as women's funerary and dance overskirts or long ceremonial wrappers worn by men and women, being assembled from multiple panels and borders sewn together. Among Kuba textile makers, this constructivist approach, combined with locally developed techniques of cut-pile embroidery and appliqué decoration, generated a kinetic design process that fostered change and variety across the surface. Ingenious pattern combinations

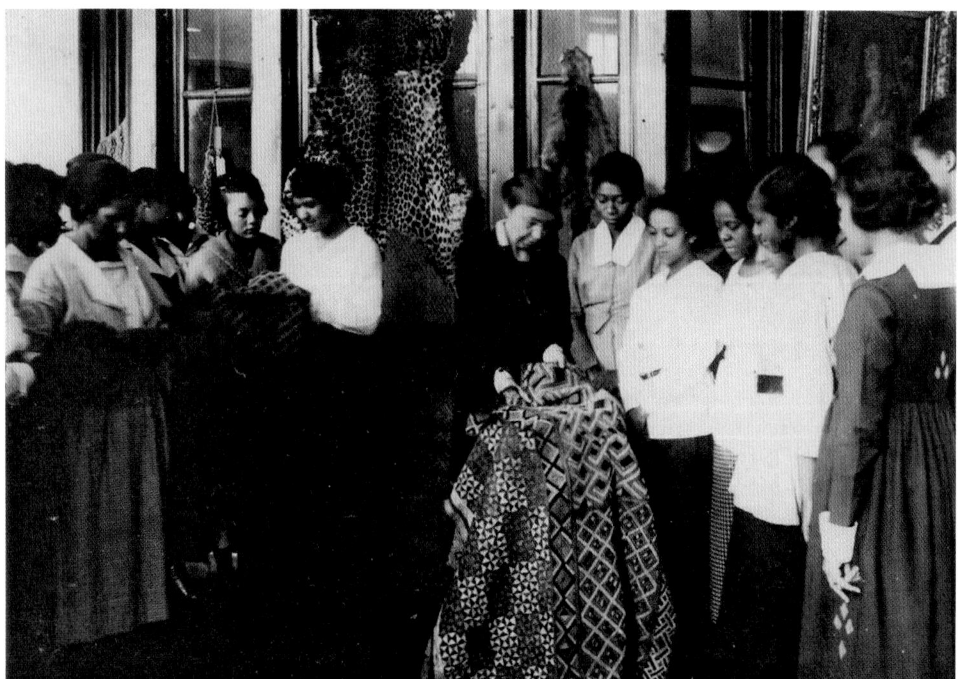

and improvisational contrasts of texture, line, shape, scale, and symmetry, combined with intense variability of detail, became the defining characteristic of Kuba textile design.

These attributes are especially associated with Shoowa women—exceptional pattern innovators and virtuoso needleworkers within a larger tradition of skilled textile artistry. Shoowa textiles were among the first Kuba artifacts collected in the early 1880s, mostly as adjuncts to the first colonizing, trading, and missionary expeditions exploring the Kasai region.[6] While receptive to the variety and fine execution of the raffia cloths, few Westerners of the time inquired into their cultural significance or methods of fabrication. Most likely the textiles were obtained at trading posts along the rivers where male outsiders probably had limited access to the women who made them—and even less familiarity with the methods or materials employed.

On the cusp of the major transformation wrought by colonization, this loss of historical information about indigenous textile practice and knowledge is significant. A notable exception, Patricia Darish observes, was a Belgian official, Adolphe de Macar, whose perceptive observations about the textiles' funerary usage, and the similarity between Kuba symbols and women's scarification markings, were substantiated by later research. Textiles that Macar acquired circa 1883 were foundational to the Congo collections amassed for King Leopold's colonial museum at Tervuren, Belgium.[7]

It fell to the African American missionary William Sheppard (1865–1927) to obtain additional firsthand information while assembling the first American collection of Kuba art. In an intrepid journey undertaken in 1890, Sheppard had dared to breach the borders of the Kuba kingdom which had long been barred to outsiders. His subsequent relationship with the Bushong ruler and royal clan ended decades of isolation and yielded a trove of late nineteenth-century textiles and artifacts that were acquired by Hampton University Museum in 1911 (fig. 1).

The objects played an important role in the artistic and craft education of Hampton students, including the artist John T. Biggers who returned decades later to paint two murals for the university library. *House of the Turtle* (1992) features a background of black and white triangle motifs, a patterning device that in other Biggers works, such as *Starry Crown* (1987), is

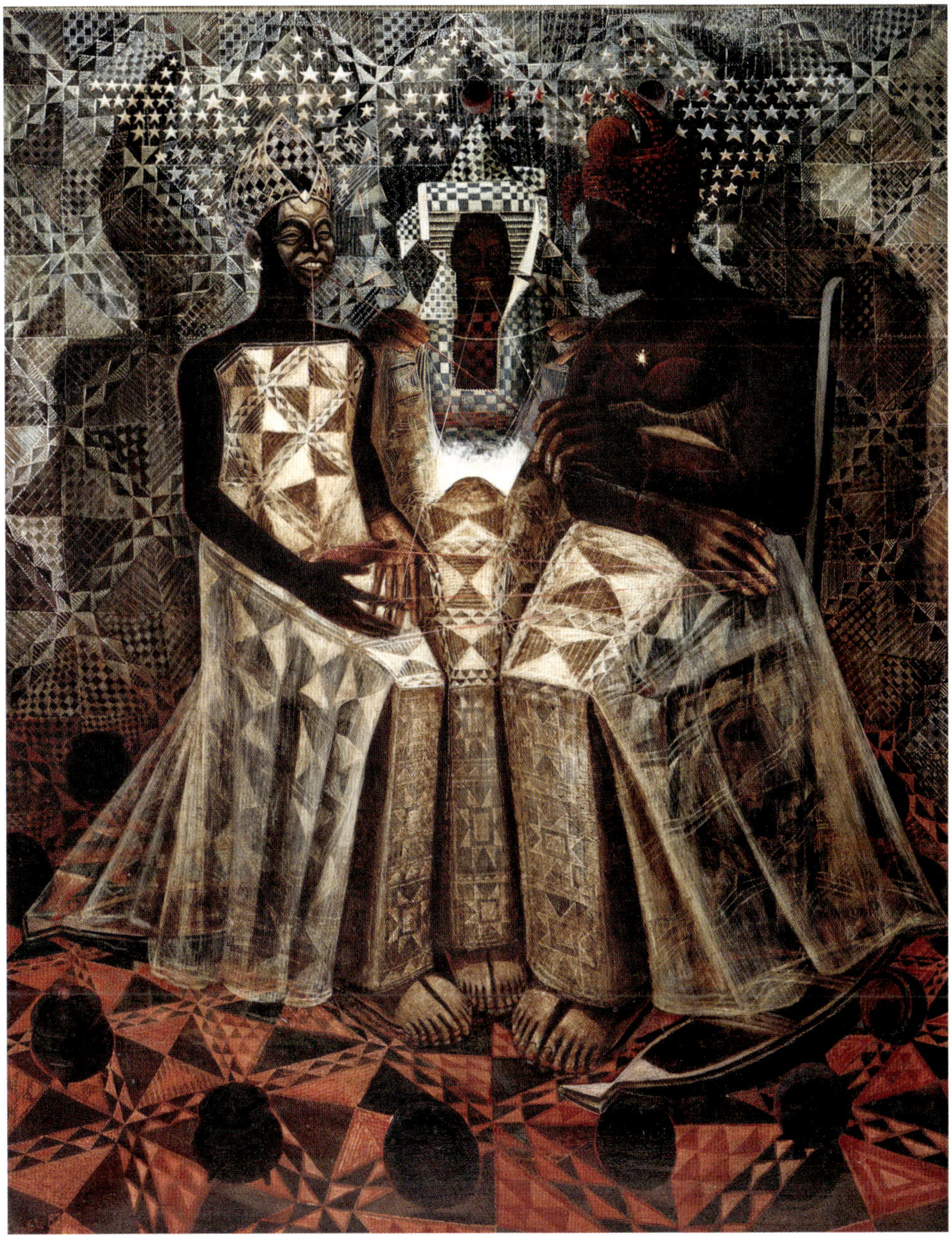

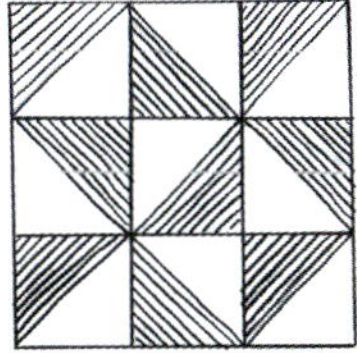

Fig. 2 (left)
John T. Biggers (1924–2001),
Starry Crown, 1987. Acrylic and
mixed media on Masonite, 60⅛ ×
48⅛ inches (152.7 × 122.2 cm).
Dallas Museum of Art

Fig. 3 (above)
Lantshoong motif, adapted from
Joseph Cornet, *Art Royal Kuba*.
Milan: Edizioni Sipiel, 1981

associated with African American quilting traditions and socio-cultural memory (fig. 2). Here, the design also evokes the major Kuba *lantshoong* emblem, characteristic of Congolese raffia panels and an elite woman's overskirt pieced from dyed bark cloth found among Sheppard's collection (fig. 3).

Refractions

Kuba geometric abstraction, its asymmetries, and fractal graphics have come into focus in recent decades as commercial fabrics decorated with Kuba patterns, as well as modern examples imported from the D R Congo, have pervaded the global market. Yet even as the brilliance of African design is increasingly visible, the identification of this singular visual theme has largely eluded art historians in comparison to the ever-widening conversation about Western modernism's debt to African art.[8]

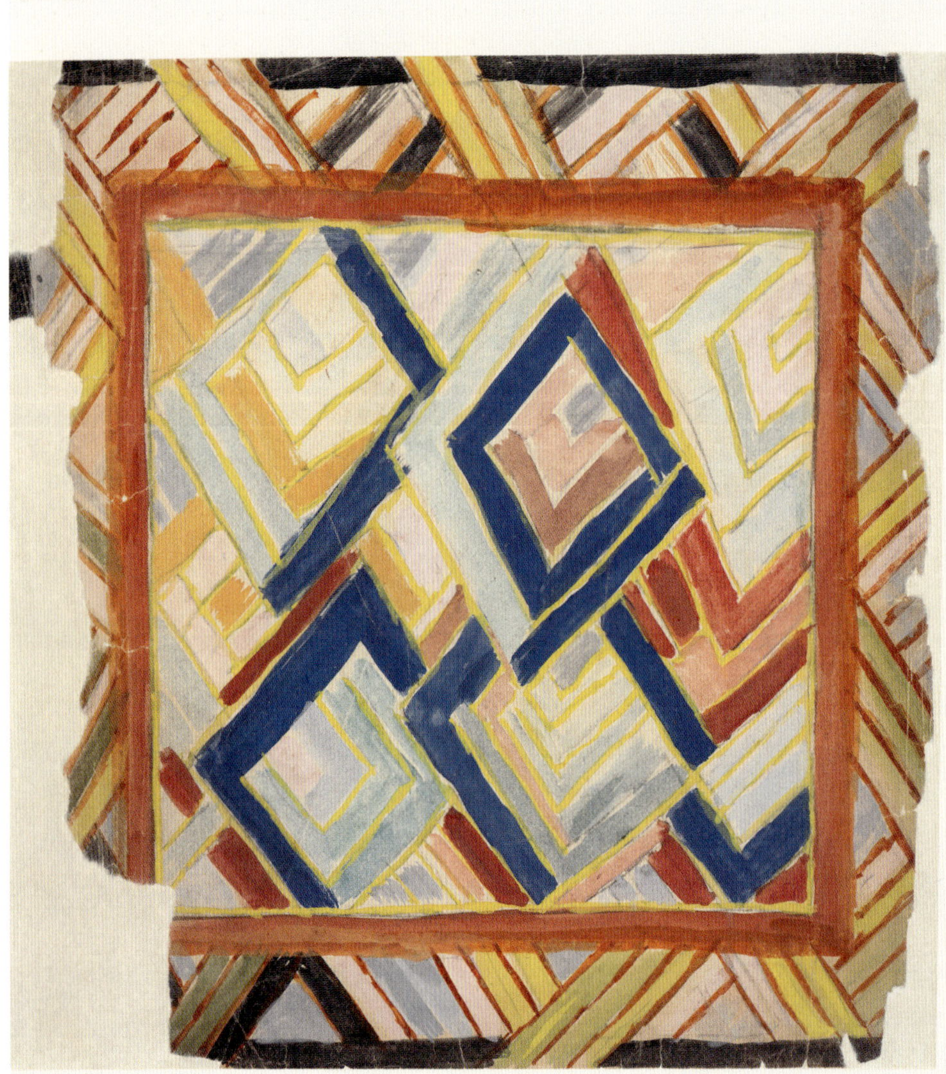

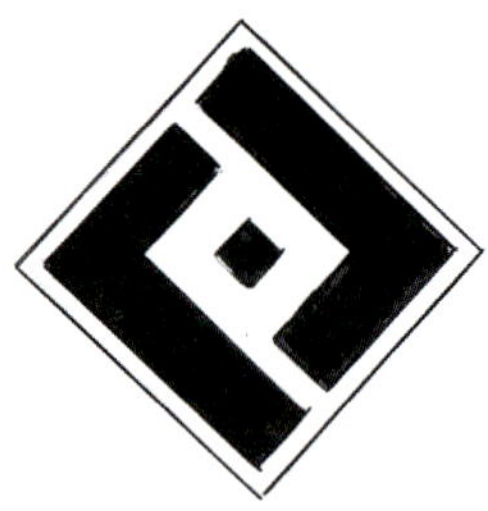

Fig. 4 (left)
Omega Workshops (Duncan Grant and/or Vanessa Bell), Rug Design, 1913–15. Graphite and body color on wove paper, 20 × 20 inches (50.8 × 50.8 cm). Accession no. D. 1958. PD. 21. The Courtauld Gallery, London

Fig. 5 (above)
Woto or *Woot* motif, adapted from Joseph Cornet, *Art Royal Kuba*. Milan: Edizioni Sipiel, 1981

Nevertheless, allusion to Kuba surface design—running the gamut from creative adaptation to outright appropriation—has been apparent since the tradition first became known outside the Congo. The cut-pile and embroidered panels included in the massive colonial importation of African cultural and artistic objects between 1890 and 1930 also began to appear in the emerging "primitive art" market in Paris, Brussels, and London. The textiles were seen and acquired by the painters, sculptors, art critics and dealers, theater designers, poets, and writers who were captivated by *l'art nègre* as well as by new exposure to Black music and dance. This "vitalizing influence," to quote Alain

Locke, percolated to craft and couture studios adjacent to this avant-garde.[9] The Cubist aesthetic, forged with ideas learned from African sculpture, melded with the design thinking evident in newly available Central, North, and West African textiles from the Francophone colonies. It was refracted into a modernist expression of the applied arts that continued to gain traction through the Art Deco period.

In London, the Omega Workshops, co-founded by the eminent curator-critic Roger Fry and the Bloomsbury artists Vanessa Bell and Duncan Grant in 1913, represent an important facet of this multi-national, and artistically liberating, design movement—and, equally, the pernicious Eurocentric omission of any ethnic attribution or source of inspiration.

Fry had closely studied Kuba art exhibited at the British Museum, which had been assiduously acquired and documented by the Hungarian ethnographer Emil Torday in dedicated collecting expeditions between 1907 and 1910.[10] Given the modernist concentration on African sculptural form at the neglect of the textile arts, Fry's remarks on the "intense and vivid plastic sensibility" of Kuba textiles are insightful for the time.[11] Indeed, he recognized that their seemingly "accidental play" of contrast and variation of surface and color embodied an underlying rhythm that he considered essential to artistic composition.[12] Today, however, the qualities of Kuba design that Fry characterized as accidental or random are better understood as exemplifying the improvisational energies and processes inherent in African textile aesthetics.

Many studies produced by the Omega artists for hand-tufted rugs and decorative fabrics to be sold at the Workshops drew on Kuba templates. While it would be reductive to view these beautiful impressionistic gouaches by Fry himself, as well as by Grant, Bell and Frederick Etchells, as simply derivative, their creators had seemingly absorbed the spontaneous thinking and making behind Kuba textiles, in addition to their eclectic geometries.

That influence is palpable in signature stylistic elements and layouts taken from Kuba panels and overskirts. Common to many Omega designs is a center section, framed with narrow borders, and inlaid with a geometric mosaic composed of interlocking chevrons, hooks, lozenges, or triangles of variable proportions. Vigorous slanted and parallel lines of uneven lengths and widths imply the textural contrast between Kuba linear embroidery and the finely sculpted dimensionality of the cut-pile blocks. The source is conspicuous in a composition attributed to Duncan Grant and/or Vanessa Bell that reproduces the format of a Torday-era piece in the British Museum, filling the field with a freeform rendering of the archetypal *Woto* symbol (fig. 4).[13] Several variants of this motif, honoring their mythical ancestor and primordial man, are found in the Kuba lexicon (fig. 5).

For reasons of aesthetic preference, spiritual belief, and cultural practice, as well as the kinds of plant materials and dyes available locally, traditional Kuba color schemes favored the natural yellow tones of undyed raffia (which darkened to tan or gold) combined with a bluish-black derived from iron-rich mud dyes. A red colorant (*tukula*) obtained from the powdered bark of the tropical hardwood *Pterocarpus spp.* was used to overdye textiles for funerary rituals, while gradations of pink, purple, yellow, and ochre were typical of the coloration of early status cloths from the northern Kasai region.

It was only in the mid-twentieth century that this palette embraced botanical and chemical shades of green, orange, and rusty red. Indigo was always rare. In the late nineteenth century, for example, valuable blue trade cloth was exclusive to royal women. In later periods, blue was sometimes obtained from typewriter inks. The vibrant colors employed by the Omega artists—all admirers of the decorative color shapes and lines in paintings by the Fauves, especially Henri Matisse, and abstractionists like Wassily Kandinsky—therefore represented a significant departure from the African prototypes.

The fusion of a painterly European color sensibility with Central African ideas of asymmetric pattern composition is similarly evident in textile designs created at the Wiener Werkstätte, founded in Vienna by the architect Josef Hoffmann in 1903. The applied arts were integral to the Werkstätte vision of a unifying design aesthetic encompassing the entire built environment from outside in, shaping architecture, interior decoration, artwork, and domestic furnishings and objects.[14] There are obvious parallels with the Omega Workshops' creative mission expressed through the dress and homes of the eccentric Bloomsbury group, although the Werkstätte's luxurious products enjoyed greater commercial success among the Viennese social elite.

Vienna did not house the extensive Kuba collections assembled elsewhere in Europe, but a Shoowa woman's overskirt, likely obtained during the first expedition along the Kasai River, had been acquisitioned by the Imperial Ethnographic Museum at the notably early date of 1887.[15] Interest in African textiles was soon manifest among the artistic circle surrounding the Secessionist painter Gustav Klimt and the fashion designer Emilie Flöge. Verena Traeger has investigated potential visual affinities between Kuba patterning and the shimmering cascades of ornamental elements in garments depicted in Klimt's renowned compositions from his Golden Period. Klimt was well acquainted with African

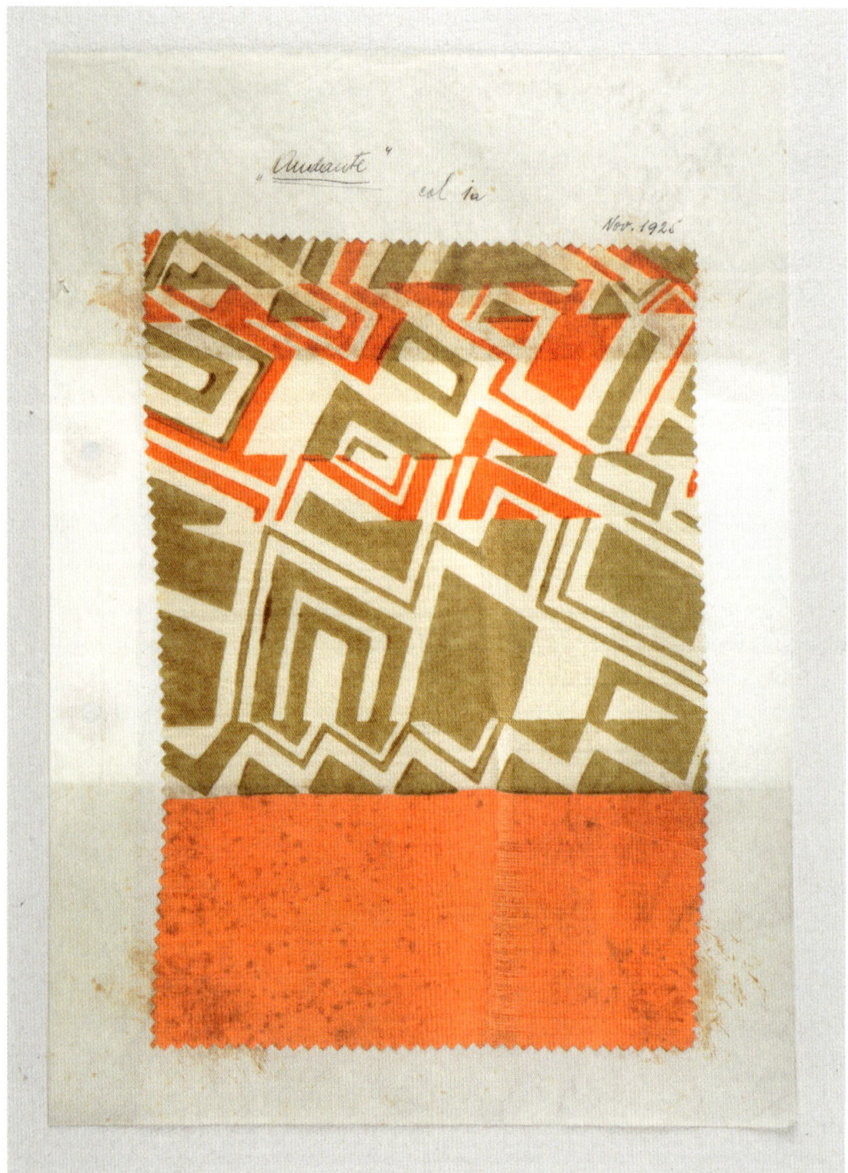

Fig. 6 (left)
Mathilde Flögl, *Andante*, 1925.
Fabric swatch, silk, printed,
dimensions unknown. Inventory
no. WWS 34. MAK – Museum of
Applied Arts, Vienna, Austria

Fig. 7 (opposite)
Sonia Delaunay, *Écharpe* (scarf),
"Simultaneous fabric" no. 70,
1924. Crêpe de chine, wood block
printing, two colors, 18½ × 55⅛
inches (47 × 140 cm). Inventory
no. 40402. Musée des Arts
Décoratifs, Paris

sculpture and is known to have visited the Congo
collections at Tervuren around 1914.[16] His association
with Brussels was, moreover, established through the
commission of the magnificent mosaic frieze executed
for the Palais Stoclet, which Hoffmann designed for
a Belgian financier (1905–11). Traeger also detects
African inspiration in the black and white checkerboard,
triangle, and striped fabrics fashioned into informal
"artistic" or "reform" dresses worn by Flöge. Since
textiles like the Kuba titleholder skirts that Traeger
cites as possible referents were mostly unknown

outside the Kasai region until much later, the correlation
remains hypothetical. The Kuba *Ngaady a Mwash* mask
portraying a mythical female ancestor whose face is
painted with black and white triangles (a design echoed
in the bark cloth overskirt) is a more likely source.

A direct link to the Kuba pattern language, however,
is discernable in some of Hoffmann's own fabric
studies. Two drawings, *Miramar* and *Ragusa*, made
between 1910 and 1915, may have been prompted by
the art on view at the Musée du Congo, located in the
same suburb as the Stoclet mansion. However, the

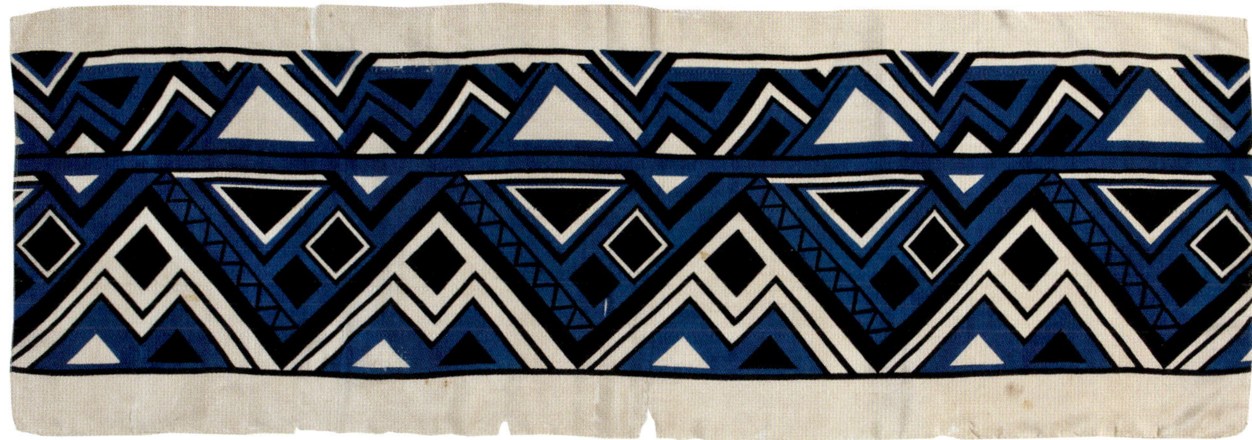

largest Werkstätte output of Shoowa-derived themes occurred between 1925 and 1931. Those sketches, executed in multiple colorways for printed silks and cottons, represent a small fraction of an inventory of 1,800 patterns devised over thirty years in the fashion and textiles department.[17]

A survey of this huge archive reveals how distinctive the noticeably "Africanized" designs truly were.[18] Outstanding women designers—Mathilde Flögl, Maria Likarz-Strauss, Mea Angerer—channeled the intricacies of Kuba abstraction with fluid creativity (fig. 6). Shoowa concepts emerge in non-repetitive, interlocking pattern formations where lines wax thick and thin, and multiple angular asymmetric shapes are staggered and complicated by shifting scales and alignments. The texturing of Kuba surfaces is implied in certain Hoffmann diagrams featuring dotted and striated geometric elements, but that unique attribute—so essential to the tactility of the raffia weave—is generally flattened in the schematics.

This decade in Vienna coincided with the maximum impact and translation of Kuba patterning into European textile and decorative arts, with Paris at the center. Developments there during the Art Deco period were echoed in Werkstätte fabrics from the late 1920s. After all, Hoffmann was the architect of the Austrian pavilion at the 1925 Parisian international exposition of decorative arts that gave the era its name. Outcroppings of influence materialized elsewhere in the European design world except, notably, at the Bauhaus where, apart from certain Kuba-inflected wall-hangings and sketches by the textile workshop's director Gunta Stölzl, and her student Gertrud Preiswerk, Kuba visual ideas apparently had limited impact.[19] Possibly this reflected the school's primary focus on weaving structures rather than on the surface effects manipulated by the Kuba embroiderers, which were readily transferable to textile printing techniques.

Reverberations

By 1930, blatant replicas as well as artistic reworkings of Kuba designs were found among all kinds of French luxury goods, from fashionable ensembles, carpets, upholstery and drapery to printed papers and bindings. This florescence is abundantly documented in interior design portfolios and photographs published at the time.[20] Kuba and Art Deco geometric themes are remarkably alike in their graphic boldness and dazzling elaboration of elemental shapes. And Art Deco's mining of exotic cultural sources—Egyptian, Grecian, Indo-Chinese, and West African—is widely recognized.[21] Yet the extent to which two specific Congolese visual traditions—Kuba and Mangbetu—contributed to the style remains largely invisible to either scholarship or popular interest in the genre.

Anticipating this design phenomenon, however, a decided Kuba modality propels the jagged rhythms of textile creations made by the versatile and experimental artist Sonia Delaunay, starting around 1923. The generously sized scarves and shawls shown in portraits by her artist husband Robert Delaunay, depicting the Dadaist poet Tristan Tzara and others within the couple's avant-garde orbit, were the nucleus of an extensive collection of block-printed and embroidered

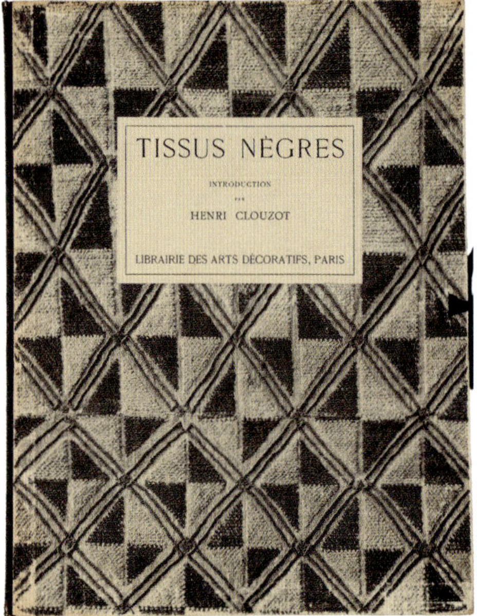

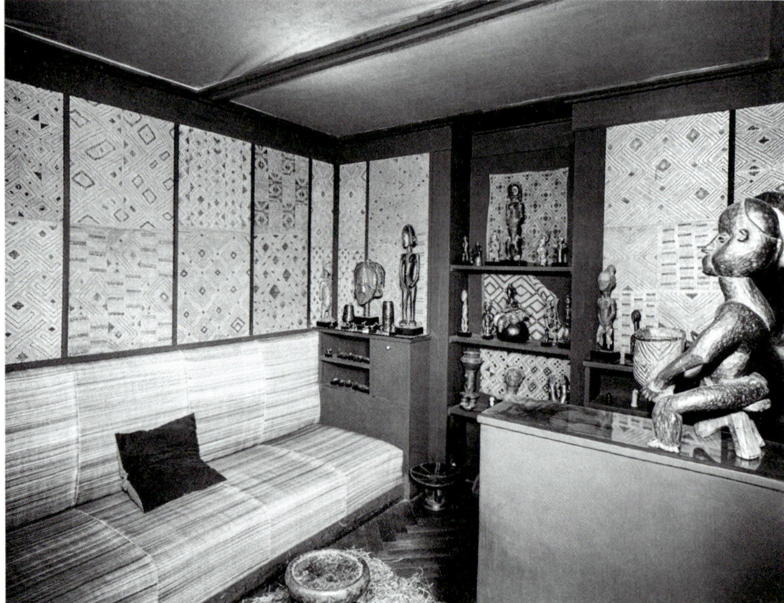

Fig. 8
Henri Clouzot, *Tissus nègres*,
cover. Paris: Librairie des Arts
Décoratifs, 1931. Courtesy Andrés
Moraga. Photo: Scott McCue

Fig. 9
Heinrich Kulka (photographer),
*House for Tristan Tzara (reception
room), Montmartre, Paris*, ca. 1930,
from Heinrich Kulka, *Adolf Loos.
Das Werk des Architekten*. Vienna:
Löcker Verlag, 1979 (reprint)

clothing and fabric designs that she produced under the labels of the *Atelier* and *Boutique Simultané*.

Featuring dynamic sequences articulated with sharp cubist forms and linearities moving diagonally across a plane or in sawtooth bands, the patterns marked a striking shift in visual expression from Delaunay's earlier textiles. Those styles included the amorphous patchwork assemblage of the 1913 "simultaneous dress" and embroidered and appliquéd floral motifs evoking Ukrainian and Russian folk art. Delaunay's first theatrical costumes were also more reminiscent of Commedia dell'Arte or Harlequin outfits. Others she made for the Ballets Russes' *Cleopatra* (1918) mixed fanciful Egyptian styles with rainbow curvilinear and spherical motifs that reprised the prismatic color refractions and concentric discs and arcs which had already become a hallmark of her lyrical painting aesthetic.

One of the few Delaunay fabrics given a name, as well as a number, is the "simultaneous" scarf titled

"African art," which Jacques Damase, the custodian and promoter of her artistic legacy, notes was inspired by "l'art nègre"[22] (fig. 7). Sherry Buckberrough has linked the "African angles" and "bold tonal contrast" of Delaunay's designs during this period to popular imagery of Black performers in 1920s Parisian jazz clubs and dance halls.[23] But such generalized descriptions account for neither the vast diversity of African textile cultures and styles, nor the particular impact and presence of Kuba textiles in Paris at that time.

Delaunay's great friend and dramatic collaborator, Tristan Tzara, was a noted collector of Kuba textiles. Tzara's textiles were published, along with velvets belonging to the pre-eminent "primitive art" dealers Charles Ratton and Galerie Percier, in *Tissus nègres* in 1931, the first publication to highlight the artistry and virtuosity of the tradition (fig. 8). "They fill their fabric with inspiration, without the aid of any pattern," Henri Clouzot's preface noted. "A simple interlacing of

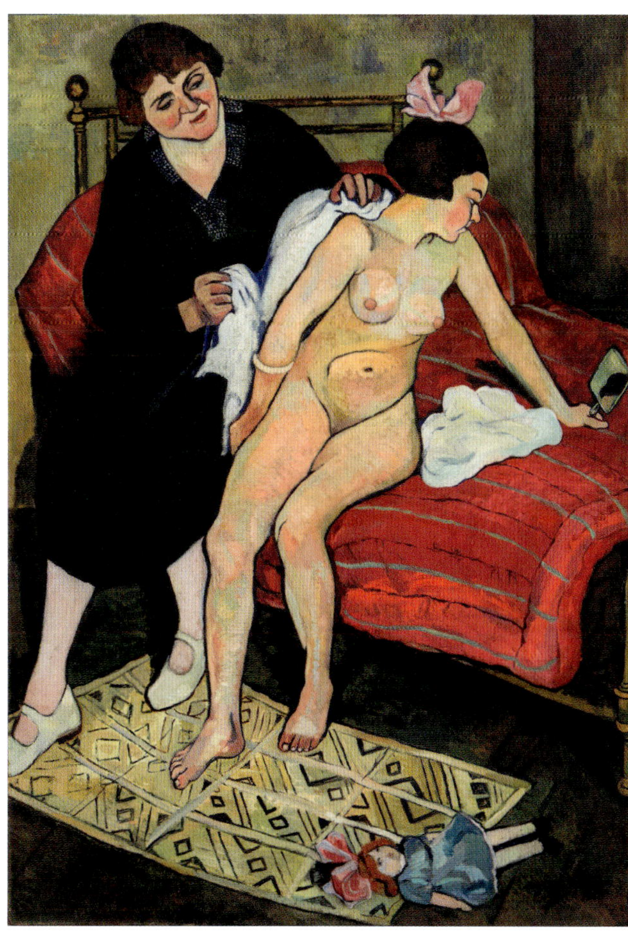

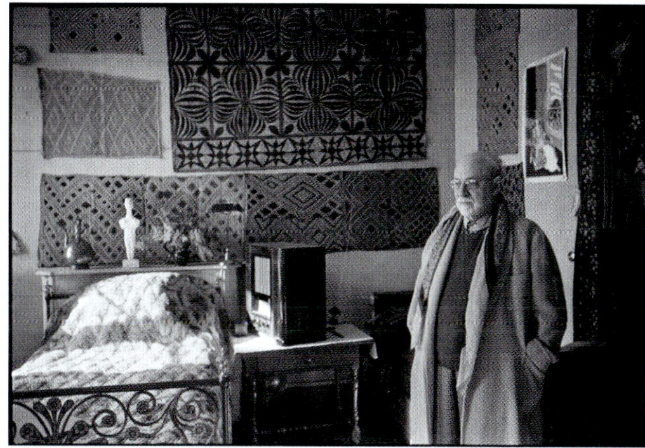

Fig. 10
Suzanne Valadon, *The Abandoned Doll*, 1921. Oil on canvas, 51 × 32 inches (129.5 × 81.3 cm). National Museum of Women in the Arts, Washington, DC

Fig. 11
Henri Cartier-Bresson, *Henri Matisse at his Villa, "Le Rêve," Vence, Alpes-Maritimes*, 1944

lines can give rise to innumerable variations either by connecting or interrupting the line, or syncopating the rhythm, like a jazz tune."[24] Tzara took further advantage of the textiles' decorative effects, lining a room in his Montmartre residence with a textured wall of Kuba prestige cloths (fig. 9).

Contemporaneous artworks similarly record the use of Kuba textiles as backdrops for African sculpture and other cultural artifacts, among them *Fétiche et Fleurs* (1926) by Palmer Hayden and *Negro Masks* (1932) by Malvin Gray Johnson—both artists involved with the Harlem Renaissance—as well as a series of photographs Man Ray made in 1930 for the socialite collector Nancy Cunard (also a patron of Delaunay's "Simultaneous" clothing).[25]

The syncopated Kuba patterns visible in Man Ray's montages, Wendy Grossman notes, linked his images with the visual idiom of Art Deco. Yet these American artists clearly had different objectives. Man Ray's

aesthetic was integral to modernist and formalist perceptions of African art, simultaneously viewed as exotic and deracinated. Kuba textiles played only a supporting role for their scintillating graphics and as outstanding examples of indigenous craft.

Hayden's foregrounding of a Kuba textile and a Fang sculpture within the traditional still-life genre, and Johnson's equally emblematic pairing of raffia cloth and African masks, on the other hand, resonated with the mission articulated by philosopher Alain Locke. Locke advocated for Black artists to locate their own version of modernism in the "ancestral legacy" and iconography of African art—among which he extolled the "superb designs of the Bushongo."[26] Kuba and other African textile patterns subsequently appear in works by several influential artists (Elizabeth Catlett, Loïs Mailou Jones, James A. Porter), signifying an African American identity aligned with this heritage.[27] Faith Ringgold's 1960s series, *The Black Light* paintings, which utilized the geometry of Kuba motifs as a structural framework and symbolic underpinning for polyrhythmic, quadripartite color forms, similarly speaks to this idea in a very different era of civil rights, feminism, and social activism.

Kuba textiles sparked differing aesthetic responses among other Western modernists. Paintings by Suzanne Valadon depict Kuba velvets in domestic settings. Her still lifes, like Hayden's and Johnson's, convey appreciation for the materiality of the raffia cloth. But the Kuba cloth cast on the floor in the intimate scene represented in *The Abandoned Doll* (1921) suggests her greater interest in the object as an isolated decorative component of the larger picture than as an autonomous indigenous artwork (fig. 10). Georges Braque did something similar with the fractured, overlapping planes of Cubism. A series of still lifes painted between 1920 and 1939 (for example, *Guitar and Pipe (Polka)* and *Vase, Palette, and Mandolin*) mixed and inter-layered fragmentary images of Kuba textiles into collage-like assemblages of distinctively patterned blocks and decorative forms.[28]

Matisse, by contrast, drew on Kuba abstraction in a more conceptual way. Kuba status cloths were pinned to the walls of all his studios amid his own paintings and the variety of world textiles that had profoundly shaped his aesthetic (fig. 11). Despite hints of Kuba elements in certain paintings,[29] Matisse never depicted the panels as he did other textiles. Yet the "endless fascination" with which he responded to their "instinctive geometry" informed his thinking and creative method.[30] Although a connection between the paper cut-outs and Kuba appliqué styles is often assumed, the true stimulus to Matisse's imagination, John Mack argues, were the cut-pile embroideries, as the title of his 1947 composition *Les Velours* implies. The spontaneity of Shoowa design, and the exploratory means by which Kuba embroiderers build their patterns block by block, were instrumental to Matisse's investigation of contour and shape, and his improvisatory arranging of color forms in the paper cut-outs of his later career.[31]

Simultaneity

Sonia Delaunay was well acquainted with most of these avant-garde artists; besides, exposure to African design was inescapable in the Paris she inhabited. Important couturiers of the period (Poiret, Schiaparelli, Vionnet, Chanel) refashioned African patterns for attire that

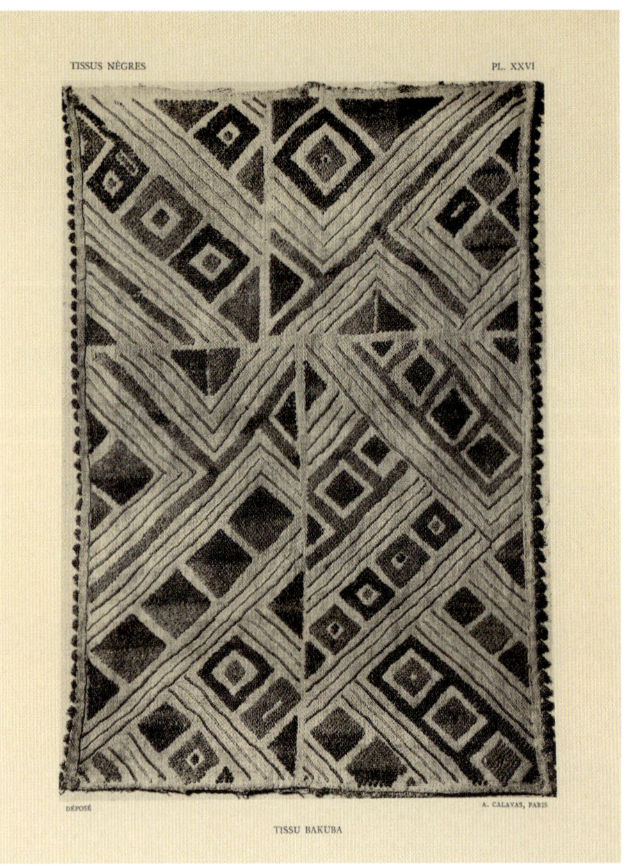

Fig. 12a
Henri Clouzot, plate XXVI from
Tissus nègres. Paris: Librairie des
Arts Décoratifs, 1931

became synonymous with the image of the modern woman.[32] Ferdinand Léger's masquerade costumes and stage décor for the 1923 Swedish Ballet's *The Creation of the World*, based on Delaunay's close friend Blaise Cendrars's retelling of an African genesis myth, exploded in a medley of cubist and primitivist visual themes sourced among African textiles and sculpture. This web of personal connections suggests, moreover, that Delaunay must have been well aware of the unique pattern aesthetic of Kuba textile art.

While the artist insisted that her primary artistic concerns were color and rhythm, the striking similarities between the vocabulary of shapes and ideas for textile composition developed by Kuba embroidery

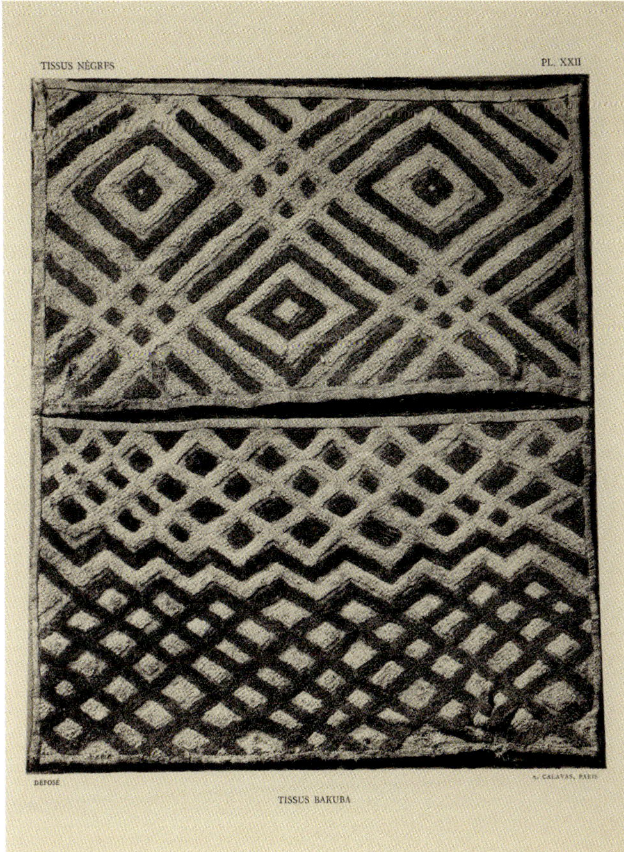

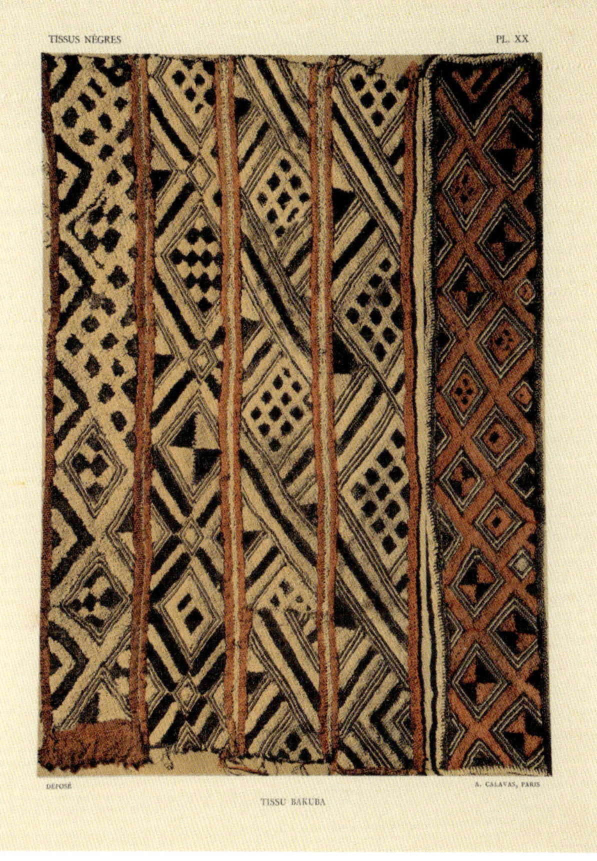

Fig. 12b
Henri Clouzot, plate XXII from
Tissus nègres. Paris: Librairie des
Arts Décoratifs, 1931

Fig. 12c
Henri Clouzot, plate XX from *Tissus
nègres*. Paris: Librairie des Arts
Décoratifs, 1931. Courtesy Andrés
Moraga. Photo: Scott McCue

artists and Delaunay's pattern schemes are more than coincidental.[33] In a concentrated period between 1922 and 1926, Delaunay generated dozens of geometric designs featuring jazzy arrangements of triangle, zigzag, and diamond motifs, both for her own enterprise and on commission for French fabric manufacturers. The material represents a small portion of her ultimately huge textile oeuvre, although she continued to play with iterations of these motifs, which were applied to jackets, shirts, fur coats, scarfs, hats, bathing suits, theater costume, and other apparel throughout the 1920s.

What brands these patterns as Kuba, rather than generically African-inspired? Or what differentiates them from contemporaneous Constructivist or Futurist designs? Or, indeed, how do they differ from any other world tradition of geometric decoration based on conventional forms?

Kuba abstract composition was developed by generations of women over centuries of intuitive graphic innovation within a collective design heritage. The style unfolded on a continuum. Bushong textiles, made for the royal clan, are the epitome of subtlety, favoring monochrome and uniform repeating shapes. Shoowa artistry, at the opposite pole, cultivates an astonishing degree of irregularity, multiplicity, and asymmetries of form. Other Kuba groups, such as the Ngongo and Ngeende, developed unique styles within this spectrum of variation.

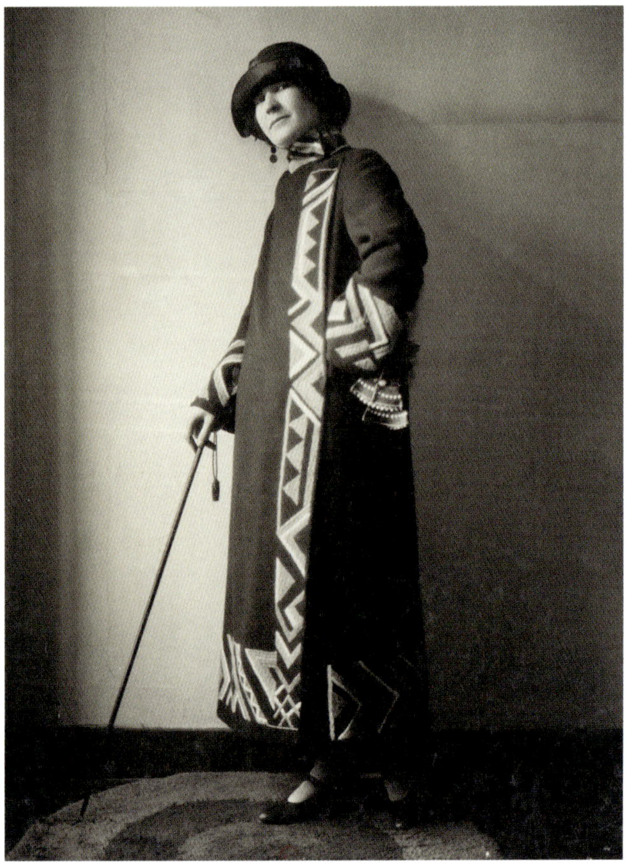

Fig. 13
Thérèse Bonney, *Miss Bonney with
a Cane (Miss Bonney à la canne)*,
self-portrait, 1924. Bibliothèque
Nationale de France, Paris

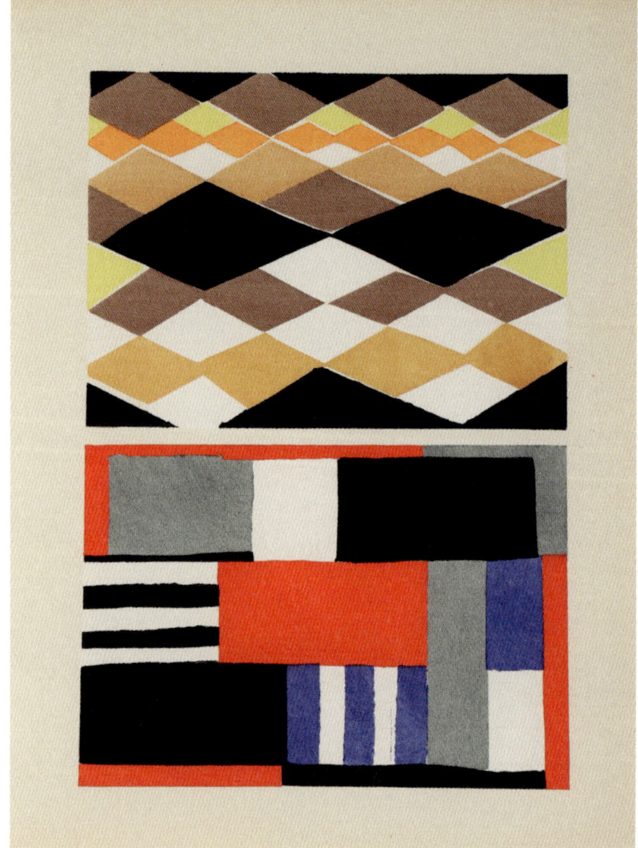

Fig. 14
Albert Morancé, *Maquettes pour
impressions sur tissus par Sonia
Delaunay*, plate 67 from *Encyclopédie
des métiers d'art. Décoration Moderne*,
vol. 2. Pochoir. Paris: Éditions Albert
Morancé. Private collection

The basic unit of design is loosely stable: a V or L
shape, hook or loop, chevron, triangle, or halved or
quartered diamond, outlined with flat stitching. Certain
configurations, while not necessarily unique to Kuba
art, have particular symbolic or cultural connotations.
The relative size or position of each motif is, however,
less fixed and subject to sudden change. Unpredictable
digressions and permutations of line and form enrich
pattern schemes or break sequences of repeating/
opposing elements. Interspaces crackle with small
accents of color difference, exploiting the flexibility
afforded by the pile technique whereby each cut fiber
functions like a single pixel and a cluster of color tufts

can yield any desired shape. Inventive fractal and
optical effects—expanding/shrinking geometries,
positive/negative interchanges, subdividing/multiplying
blocks—lead to spontaneous re-arrangements and
re-combinations. All this visual activity generates the
momentum and contrast that characterized Delaunay's
color exploration in every medium she tackled.

Delaunay evidently deployed these eye-catching
Kuba strategies in certain of her simultaneous fashions.
Extended configurations built with angular components
offset in size and register resembling those seen in
textiles from Tzara's and Percier's collections inspired
staggered, asymmetric, embroidered borders and

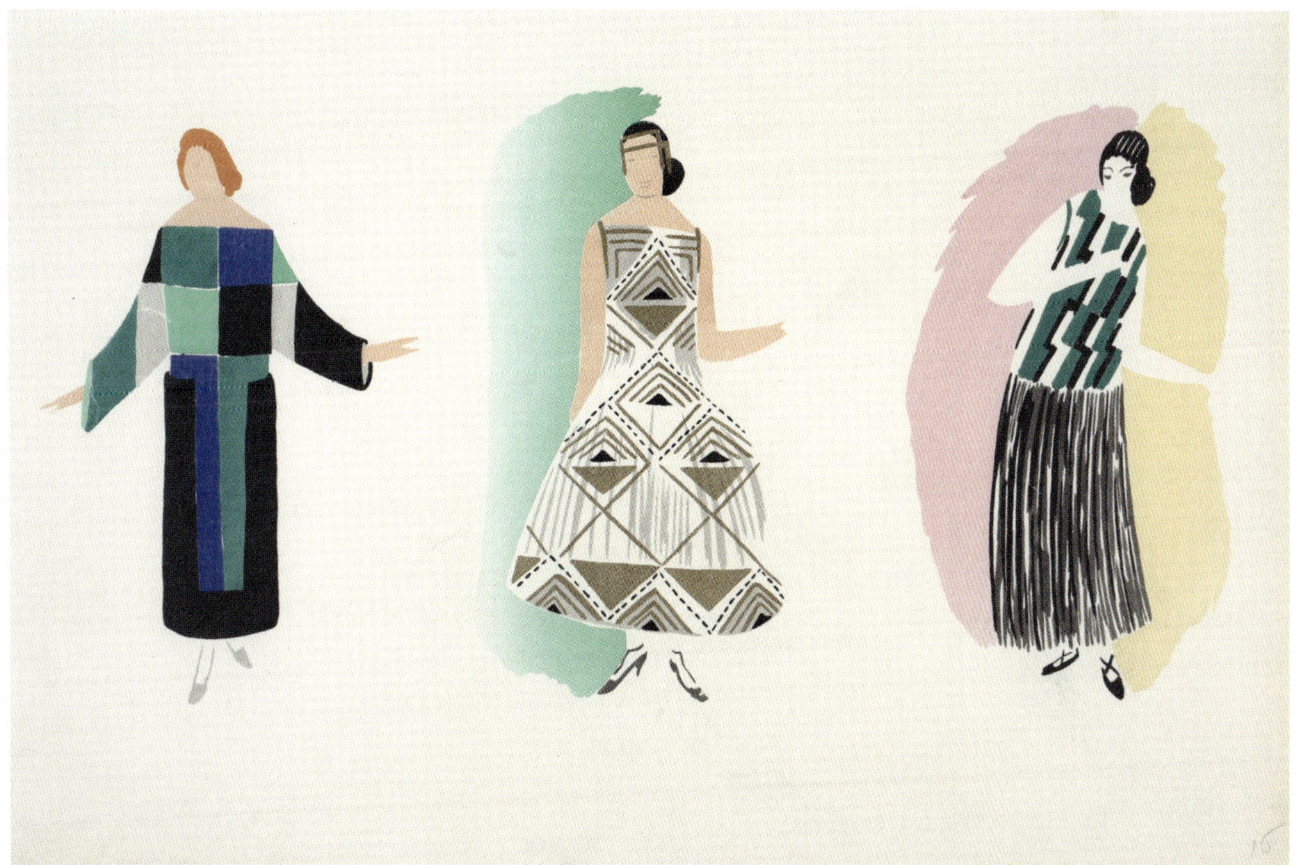

Fig. 15
Sonia Delaunay, plate 16 from
*Sonia Delaunay : Ses Peintures,
ses objets, ses tissus simultanés,
ses modes*. Pochoir. Paris: Librairie
des Arts Décoratifs, 1925

panels for dresses and coats (fig. 12 a, b, c). One version, shown in a self-portrait by the photographer Thérèse Bonney, is trimmed in the traditional format of Kuba overskirts (fig. 13). A classic pattern recycled for her Harlequin carpet or fabric adopts the flexing grids of Kuba diamond lattice and interlacing structures (fig. 14).[34] In addition, the interplay of cut-pile and embroidered textures is captured by concentric solid and striated diamond blocks, greatly enlarged in the graphics of the "African" scarf or material for a woman's evening dress (fig. 15; center).

Dimensionality, shallow depth of surface, and weight of line—fundamental Kuba properties—are likewise revealed by the carved wood blocks used for printing Delaunay's textiles (fig. 16). Transposing Kuba pattern discontinuities and juxtapositions to different planes and bodies in space, Delaunay's set designs, fashion installations, and informal studio shots posed models and mannequins in a clash of simultaneous fabrics that interacted in the kinetic totality of a Kuba composition (fig. 17).

As with her Omega and Werkstätte counterparts, Delaunay's overriding interest—and genius—was to transform these Kuba-like geometric themes with vivid color, applying her and Robert Delaunay's theories of "simultaneous contrast" to the fabrics to manipulate

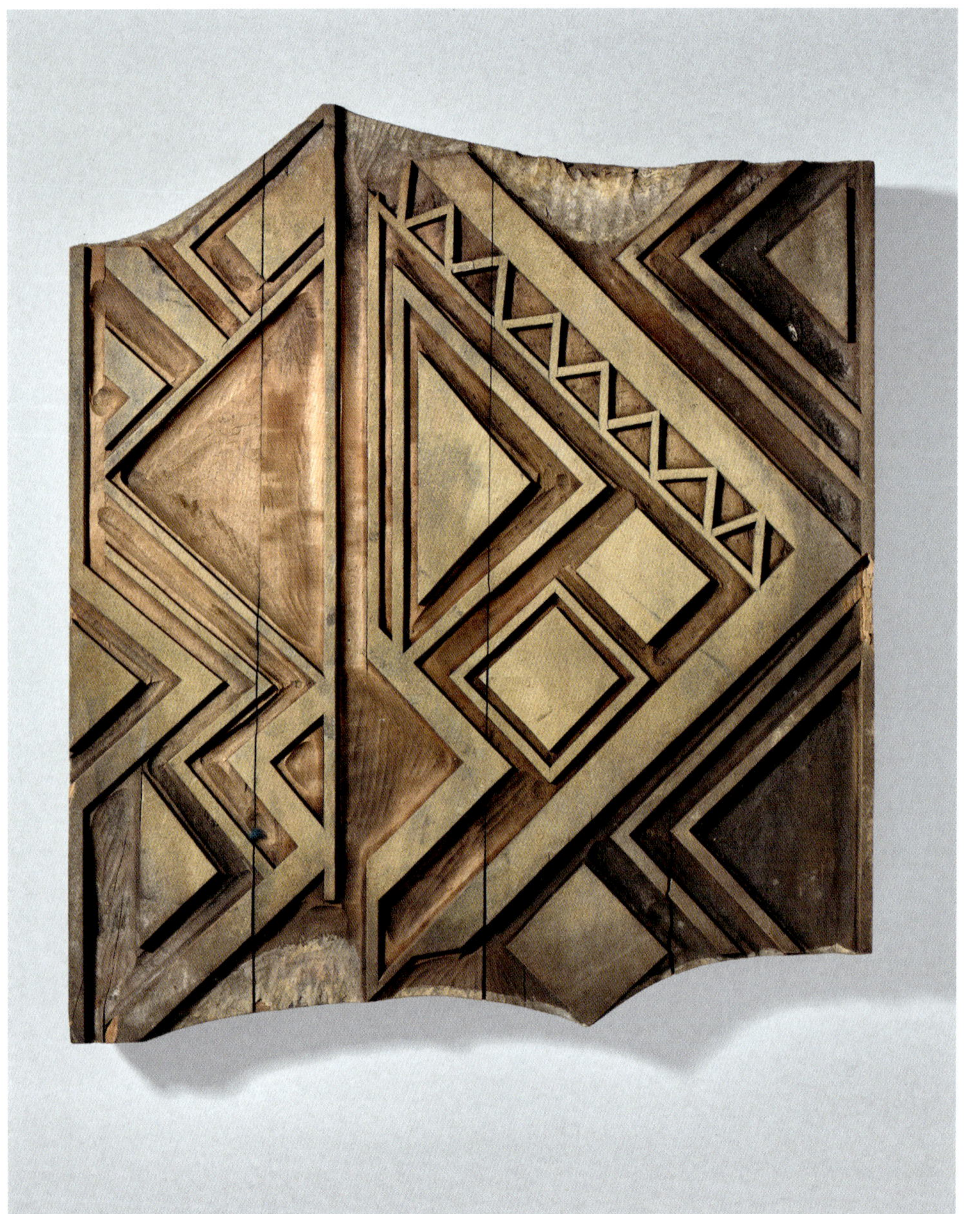

Fig. 16
Ferret Frères, printing block for
"Simultaneous fabric" no. 70, ca.
1924. Carved wood. Musée d'art et
d'histoire Paul Éluard, Saint-Denis

the optical rhythms generated by the interaction of complementary colors. Although she asserted that the simple geometric elements were merely vehicles for this process, those geometrics were recognizably Kuba.[35] Her archive, as documented in the prolific literature about the artist, yields numerous examples corroborating visual commonalities between these two genres, which were developed in such culturally diverse contexts. And it argues forcefully for the case that, even in the absence of proper cultural attribution or the artist's own reference to the tradition, Kuba textiles in particular were both inspirational and catalytic to Delaunay's practice during this productive interlude in her long career. Yet there is a felicitous convergence here: "simultaneous contrast" supplies an apt description for the Kuba aesthetic as well.

Ingenuity

Engagement with Kuba design took a different course in the United States, where curatorial and commercial

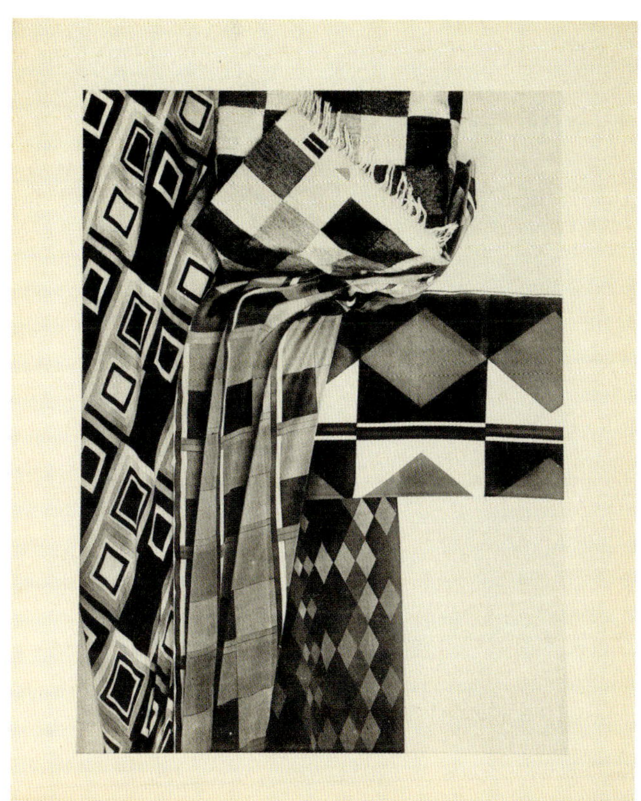

interests met in an interesting exercise in museum merchandising sponsored by the first exhibition of Congolese art at the Brooklyn Museum in 1923. Susan Hannel outlines this history in some depth, beginning around World War I, when influential figures in the design industry were motivated to revitalize the fabrication and marketing of American sportswear utilizing patterns inspired by ethnic textiles.[36] She traces the ensuing trend for "Africana" fabrics that aimed to be simultaneously "primitive" and *moderne* over several decades of adaptation, linking many fashionable creations directly to stylistic antecedents in Kuba appliqué, cut-pile, and resist-dyeing.[37]

A concerted venture centered on the 1923 exhibition, organized by the curator of ethnology Stewart Culin, an enthusiast of the arts of Congo peoples. Unlike in Europe, where the visual debt to African textile practitioners was never acknowledged, American entrepreneurial spirit saw promotional value in exploiting the apparent exotism of Congo culture—despite prevailing racist attitudes towards Africa. With an acumen that any museum shop might envy today, Culin oversaw the production of a variety of merchandise (clothing, hats, blankets, upholstery), advertised as "Congo cloth" copied from the works on display. A Bonwit Teller window display on Fifth Avenue showcased the women's dresses paired with authentic Kuba velvet panels (fig. 18). The novelty of both the museum's collection and its visual potential excited the New York papers. "The wealth of material that these textiles offer…the modern designer seems inexhaustible," wrote one critic, praising their "beautiful texture," "exquisite delicacy," and "vitality of conception and execution."[38] American fashion magazines paid attention, trumpeting the (unidentified) Kuba-influenced modes and related Kasha fabrics that appeared among the new Parisian styles.

Over a decade later, a similar flurry of international magazine articles heralded the purchase by the French-American milliner Lilly Daché of a trove of Kuba ceremonial headwear from Charles Ratton, whose ongoing professional interest in the textile arts was atypical of African art dealers or collectors.[39] Man Ray's playful photographs of this regalia, which stressed their surrealist otherness, were paired with Daché's original *"colonial moderne"* creations inspired by the headgears'

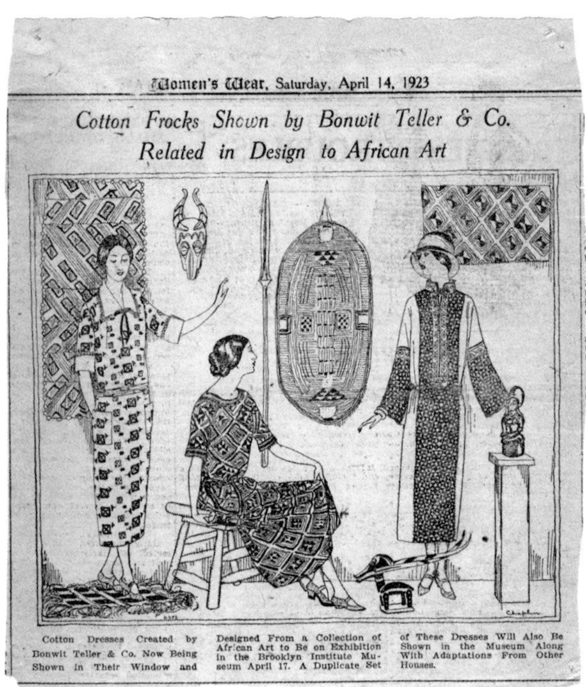

Fig. 18
"Cotton Frocks Shown by Bonwit Teller & Co. Related in Design to African Art," *Women's Wear*, April 14, 1923. Culin Archival Collection, Brooklyn Museum of Art

unusual shapes and rich decorative embellishments and beadwork.[40]

The tone of cultural superiority inflecting the *Life* and *Harper's Bazaar* commentary undermined the aesthetic impact of the images and the objects themselves— the very aspect that had motivated the Museum of Modern Art's sole exhibition of African art in 1935. Few textiles were shown, but they did include a Kuba prestige cloth, cementing that material's modernist credentials. Photographs commissioned from Walker Evans documenting the six hundred works on display similarly aligned with the institution's formalist values, although MoMA's goal of presenting the African objects as art, not ethnography, was no more culturally informed than any prior undertaking. However, one important outcome was that versions of Evans's portfolio were distributed to the historically Black colleges, exposing their faculties and students, many of whom became renowned artists and intellectuals, to the breadth of African visual expression.[41]

Kuba Modernity
The Congolese artist Djilatendo's imaginative reworking of traditional Kuba patterns into color abstractions on paper was remarkably similar to the early twentieth-century textile modernists' (fig. 19). Djilatendo/Tshela Tendu (ca. 1890–ca. 1960) has garnered renewed attention, long after his watercolors were exhibited (unbeknownst to him) in Europe in the early 1930s. Many of his exquisite compositions bear a startling resemblance to fabric sketches by Delaunay, Hoffmann, Grant, et al. Undoubtedly this accounted for their appeal at the time. However, the problematic circumstances under which the paintings were made and circulated in European art venues through the paternalistic efforts of Belgian colonialists have necessarily provoked critique.[42]

Djilatendo, a man of Lualua origin living near the Kuba village of Mweka, was reportedly a tribal chief, a tailor, an engraver, and a muralist. His artistic talent evidently led to his being encouraged (or possibly commissioned, or directed) by a Belgian, Georges Thiry, who supplied him with materials—paper, watercolors, inks—not commonly available in the Congo, in order to produce compositions for sale and display in Europe.[43] These pictorial and abstract works have been characterized as fabrications of colonial modernism.[44] However, re-situating Djilatendo's geometric compositions from the 1930s within his own cultural and visual tradition affords a different perspective. That context reveals a

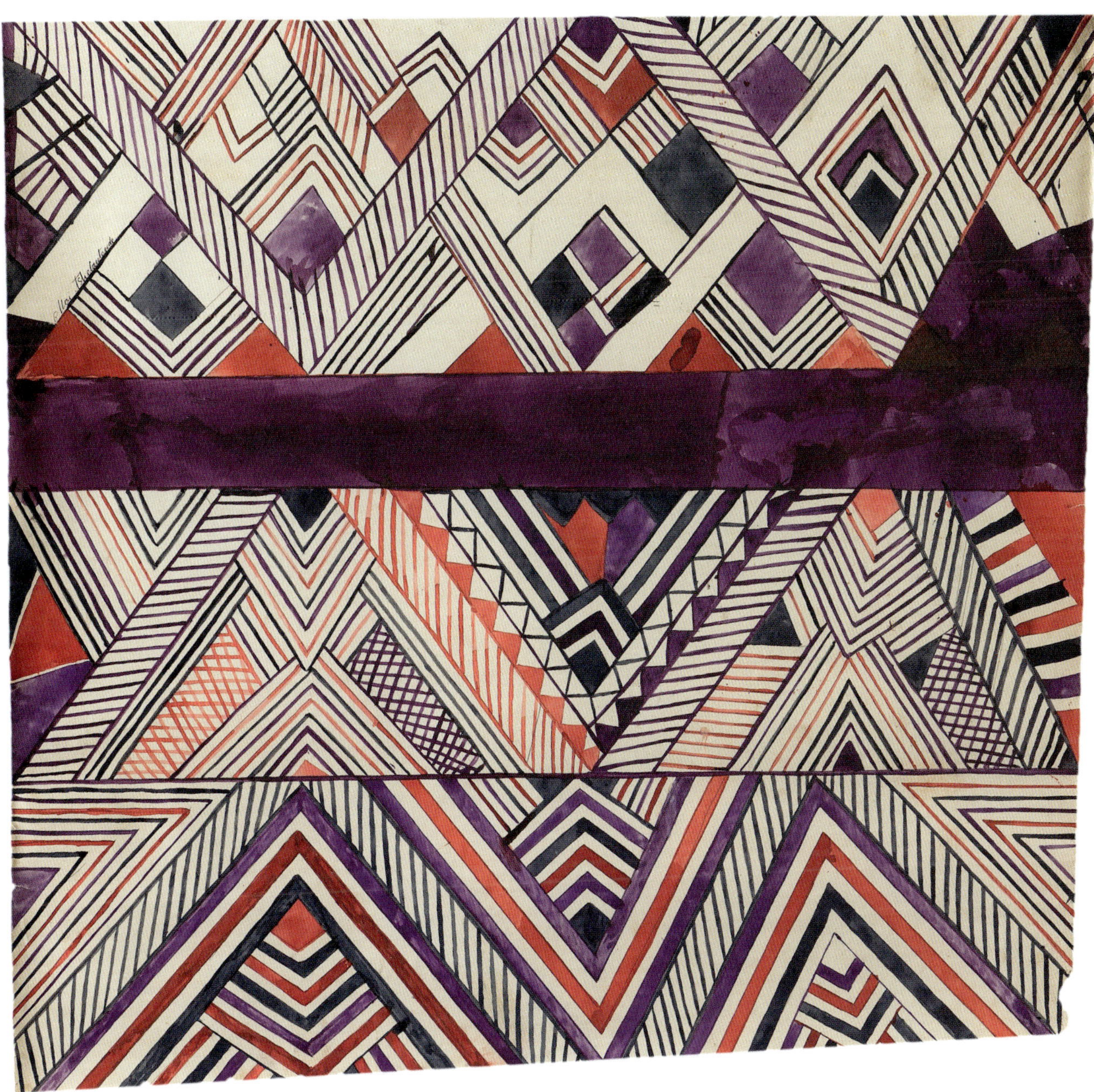

Fig. 19
Djilatendo/Tshela Tendu, *Untitled*,
ca. 1930. Watercolor and colored
inks on paper, 30⅜ × 30¾ inches
(77 × 78 cm). David Libotte
collection

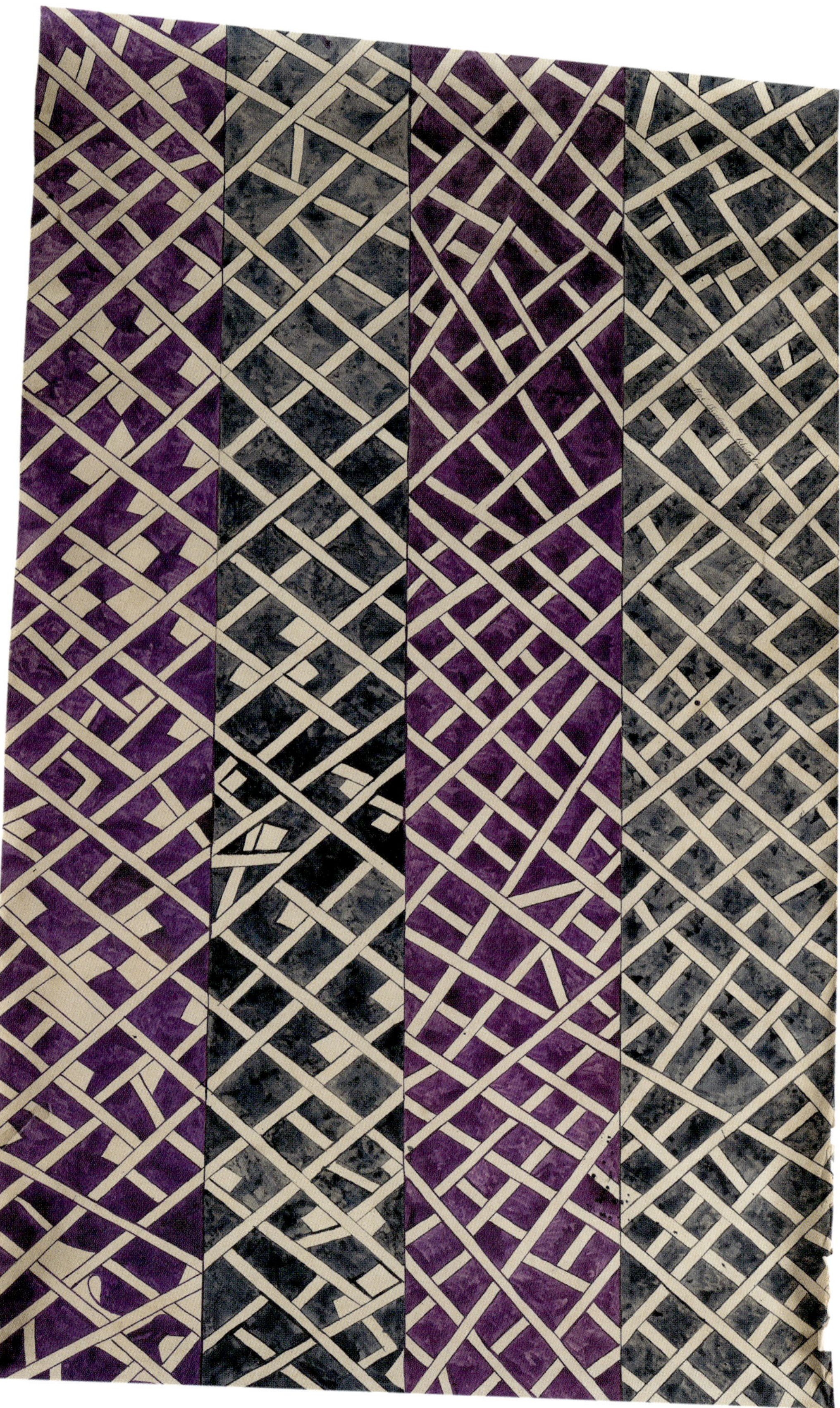

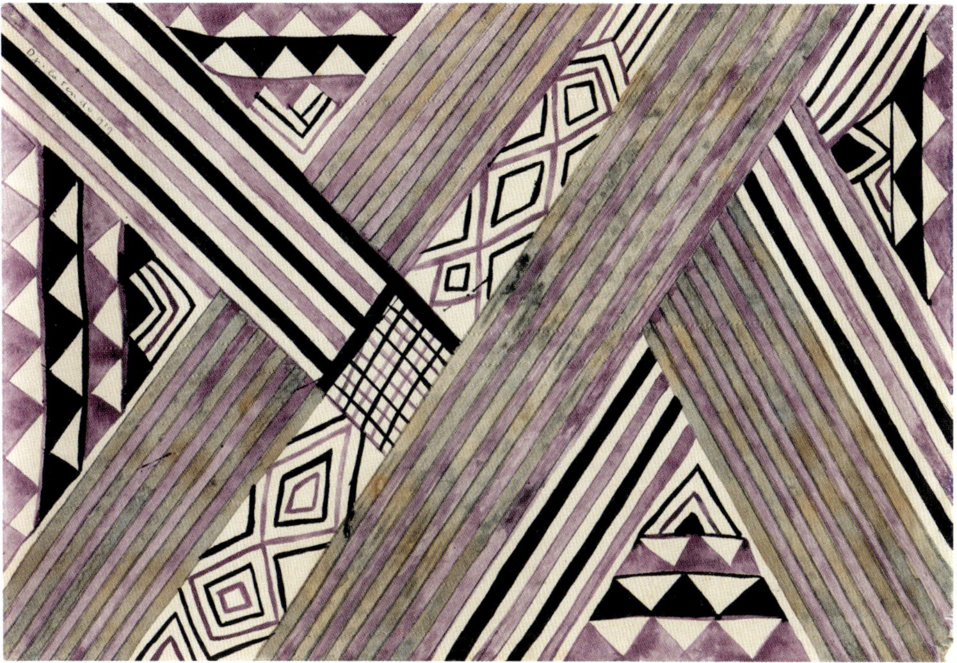

fascinating relationship to Kuba pattern creativity—in the past and going forward.

A 1929 photograph posed Djilatendo in front of a façade decorated with a Kuba mat—a flexible twined panel featuring large-scale, simplified motifs made by men.[45] Typically, textiles, or rather their surface embellishment, were women's work. But Kuba men wove the raffia ground panel and also fabricated skirts for their own use. Likewise, wood sculpture and pattern-carved status objects were masculine art forms—yet women sculpted funerary objects from hardened red *tukula* pigment with identical two-dimensional shapes and designs. This gender overlap therefore existed before Djilatendo tapped the graphic vocabulary associated with Kuba velvets for polychrome improvisations and fluid re-arrangements of Kuba patterns (figs. 20 and 21).

While his thinking about his artistic process or heritage was not recorded, presumably the visual language was imbued with cultural relevance and shaped by his immersion in the Kuba visual realm (unlike the superficially similar European modernist fashions). His freehand geometrical schemes delineating abstract forms in rhythmical progressions suggest a deep knowledge of Kuba aesthetics. Indeed, his synthesis of form and color, his breaks with—and imaginative

riffs on—conventional motifs and compositional frameworks pushed the boundaries of this art form with the free-spirited inventiveness of Kuba women textile makers. Djilatendo reportedly later applied similar designs to raffia dance skirts, foreshadowing developments in Kuba textile expression in the late twentieth century.

Kuba Continuity

Creative engagement with Kuba textiles outside the D R Congo ran underground for many decades after that first wave of attention prior to World War II. Within the Kuba sphere, however, raffia cloth retained its essential value and purpose as medium and material, and textile design enjoyed a sustained period of stylistic innovation. Public celebrations still required the display of an abundance of costume and ceremonial dress, and textiles continued to fulfill funerary, ritual, and social obligations.

A surge in production in the 1980s of Kuba cloth made for global export (rather than for local funerary and ceremonial use) responded to interest generated by international museum exhibitions and publications. This brought about certain stylistic modifications and new modes of pattern complexity, organization, and color. Purportedly, Kuba men became involved in the fabrication of cut-pile cloth, suggesting such works should probably shed the Western descriptive, "status" or "prestige" cloths, in favor of the term proposed by Patricia Darish: "design cloth," from *bwiin*, the Kuba word for design.[46] These textiles often mix graphics and formats that were once definitive of different places of origin within the Kuba kingdom. But Kuba design was never static—this late twentieth-century expression represents both a continuation of, and a resourceful spin upon, tradition.

Concurrent with this phenomenon, the Kuba aesthetic became a worldwide design trend. Applying innovative manual and industrial technologies, acclaimed designers Jack Lenor Larsen and Junichi Arai revisited Kuba templates. Larsen's translation of African textiles into contemporary cloth—always in homage to their cultural origins—reflected hands-on knowledge of ethnic weaving and craft aesthetics and techniques. This affinity informed his *Triad* fabric (1993), converting Kuba patchwork bark cloth into an undulating shadow-play of repeating dark and light triangles. Kuba tactile surface effects were also an impetus for several complexly textured fabric structures created for Nuno with Arai's revolutionary techniques and synthetic fibers.[47]

Despite the profusion of Kuba patterns in commercial applications, most companies today still do not attach the name or culture to their fabrics and consumer goods. In crediting Kuba influence on Georges Le Manach's Art Deco decorative themes for their reissue of his 1920s African portfolio, the French firm Pierre Frey is one of the rare exceptions.

The fashion world—whether couture, ready-to-wear, or mass-market—is equally remiss. One example is telling. In 1930, a Chanel dress featured a silk jersey printed with an exact copy of a Shoowa velvet overskirt; the fabric was likely produced by Rodier, whose founder had closely examined the African displays at the Parisian colonial expositions. Similarly, around 1991, Karl Lagerfeld's runway collection included an ensemble fashioned with fabric identical to a Kuba appliqué dance skirt recently on view in the exhibition *Au royaume du signe* at the Musée Dapper, Paris.

The eccentric curvilinear appliqué shapes embellishing Kuba ceremonial skirts had already infiltrated street imagery, swirling across the flowing skirt of the singer Grace Jones, as painted by Keith Haring (1987) with his graffiti-style labyrinthine lines.

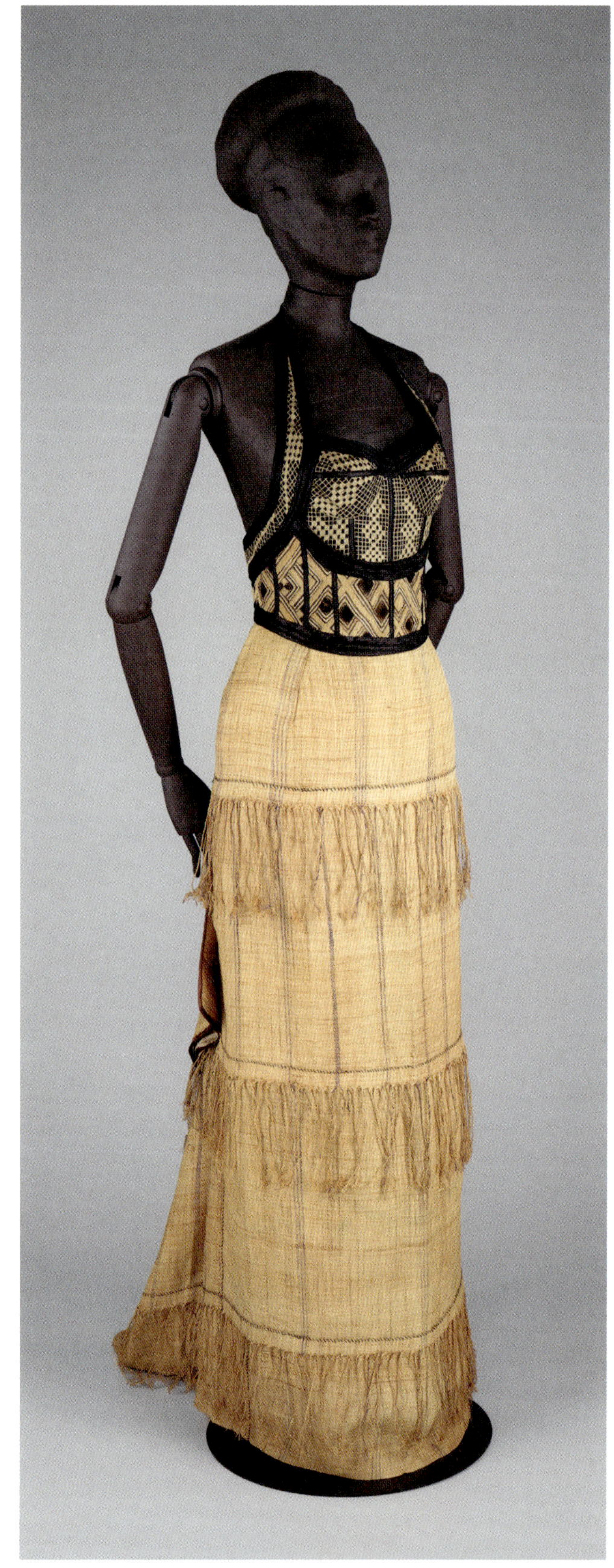

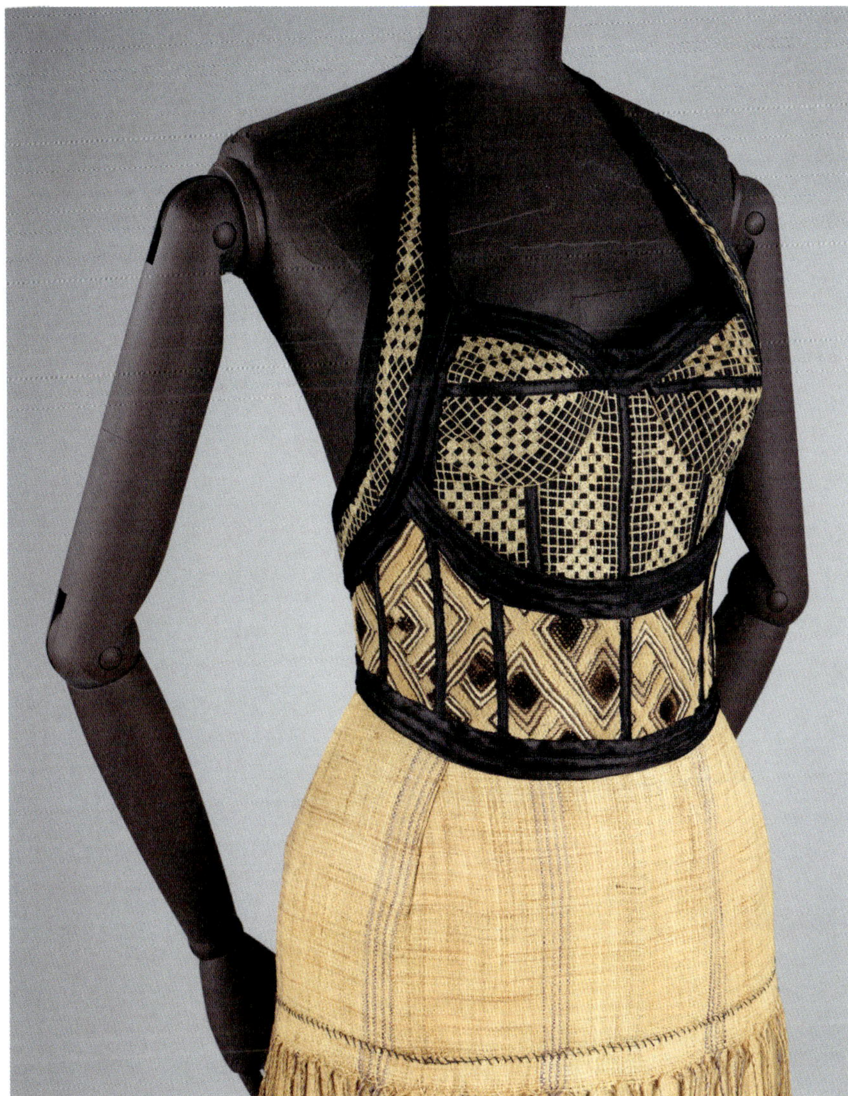

And they also caught the eye of the Black designer Patrick Kelly, who distilled Kuba appliqué in the minimalist motifs and stitching of a 1988 raffia-like linen dress. Similarly alert to his African sources, Nigerien designer Alphadi's witty assemblage of Congo materials for a 1991 garment combined fringed raffia panels with actual Kuba pile cloth (fig. 22 a, b).[48]

This discussion leaves out the great number of other designers, makers, and artists working across all media who have assimilated Kuba geometric patternmaking and its unique textural and dimensional effects. Kuba textiles have been a universal source of visual creativity for over a century. Yet this sophisticated and ingenious tradition does not enjoy the name recognition of the equally ubiquitous Kente cloth, Bogolan mud cloth, or West African wax prints that are emblematic of African diasporic image and identity. Moreover, greater attention to their potential for adaptation for multiple purposes has inevitably distanced Kuba textiles from their essential dimensions of art, ritual, culture, and history, depriving the objects of their intrinsic meaning, symbolism, and function. African art and ethnographic scholarship has in fact investigated those aspects in some depth. But the gap between the two perspectives invites a new paradigm, in which global design retrieves this context and identifies Kuba textile artists as originators and influencers of transnational scope and importance.

Illustrations

Joel Smeltzer

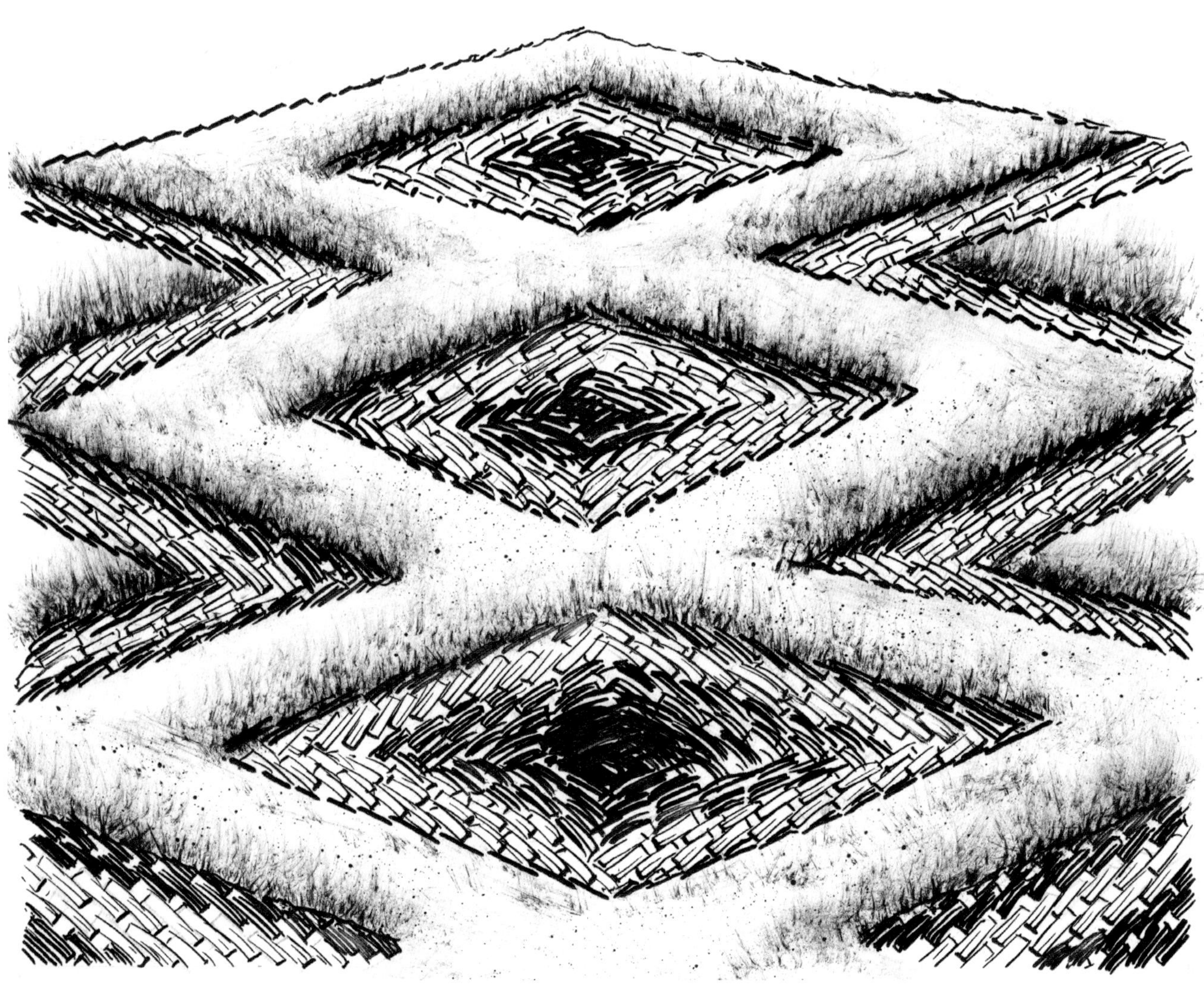

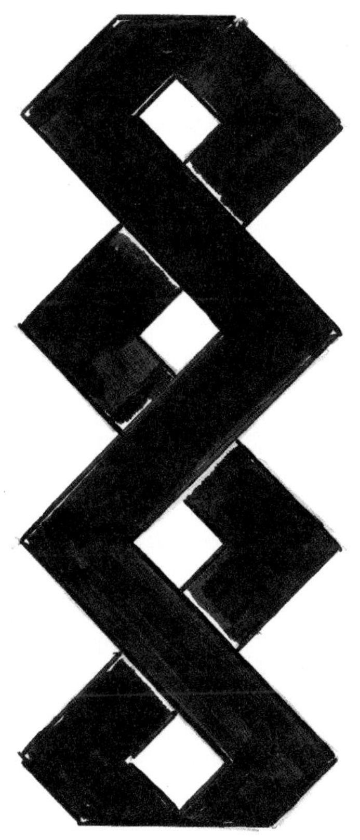

NNAAM

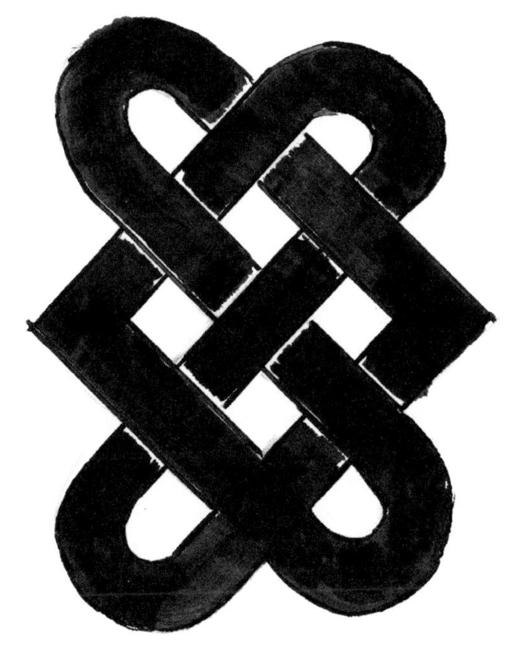

IMBOL

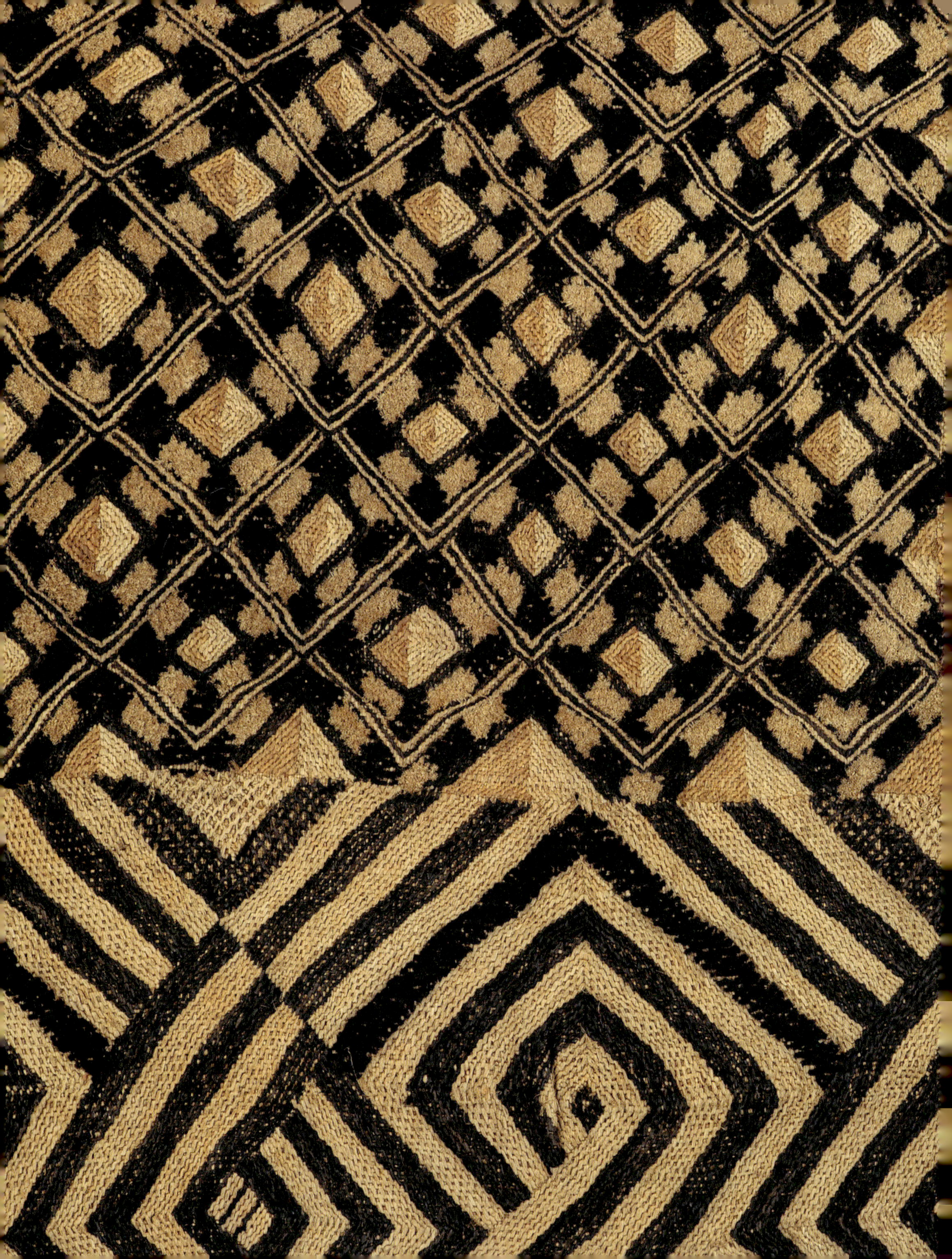

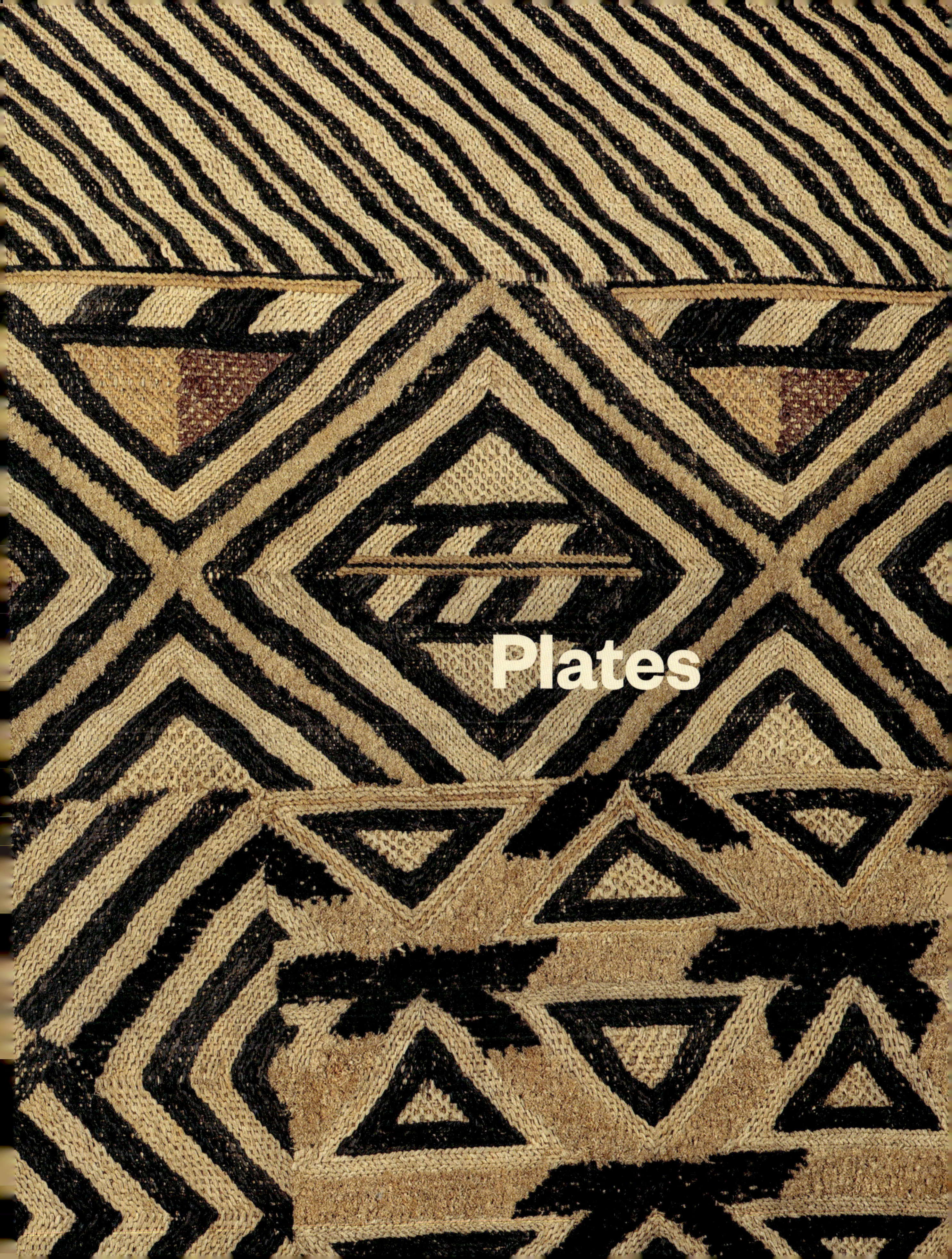
Plates

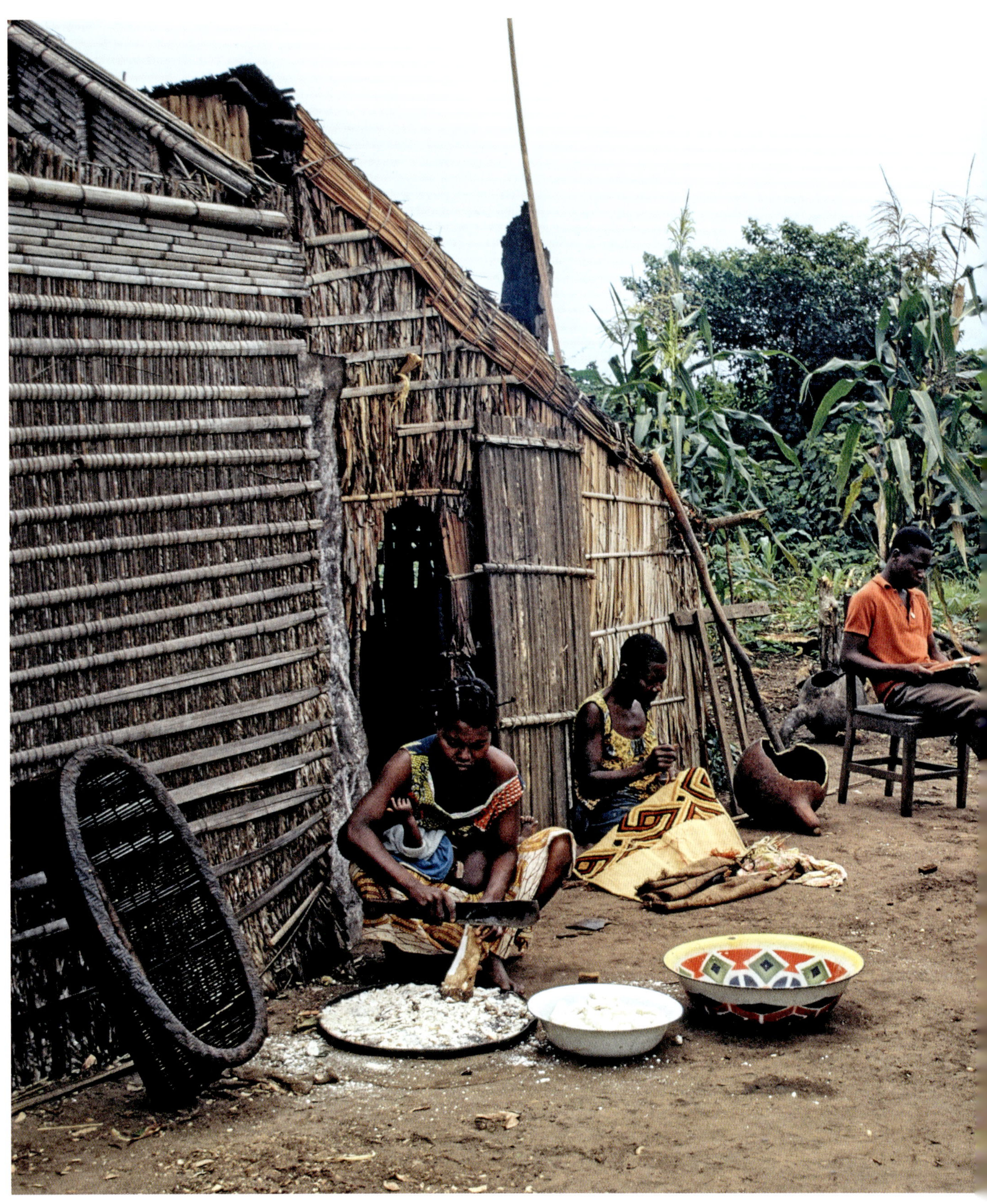

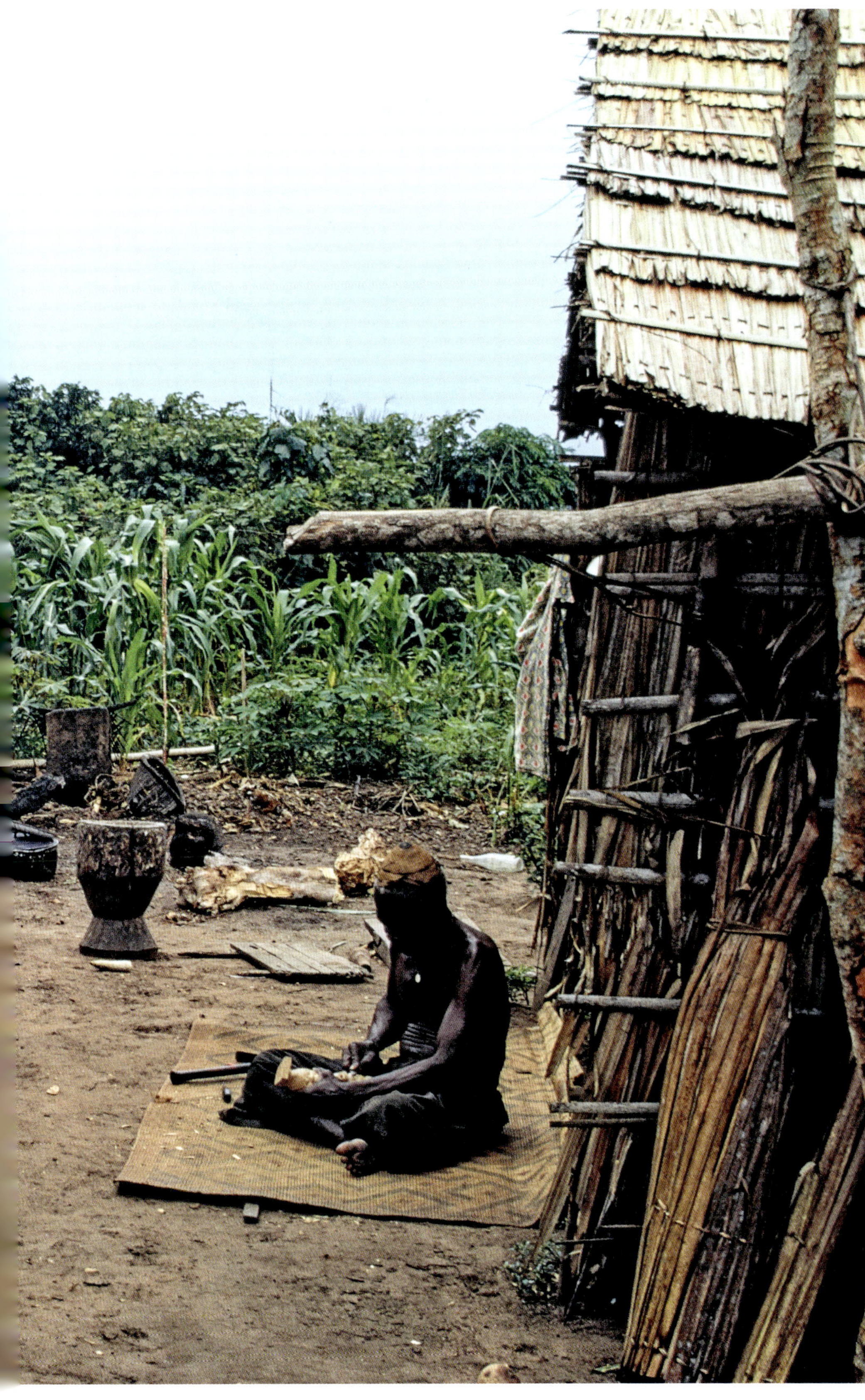

Cat. 9
Eliot Elisofon (American, 1911–1973), Domestic scenes among the Kuba people, Mushenge, Congo (Democratic Republic), 1972.
EEPA EECL 7144, Eliot Elisofon Photographic Archives, National Museum of African Art, Smithsonian Institution

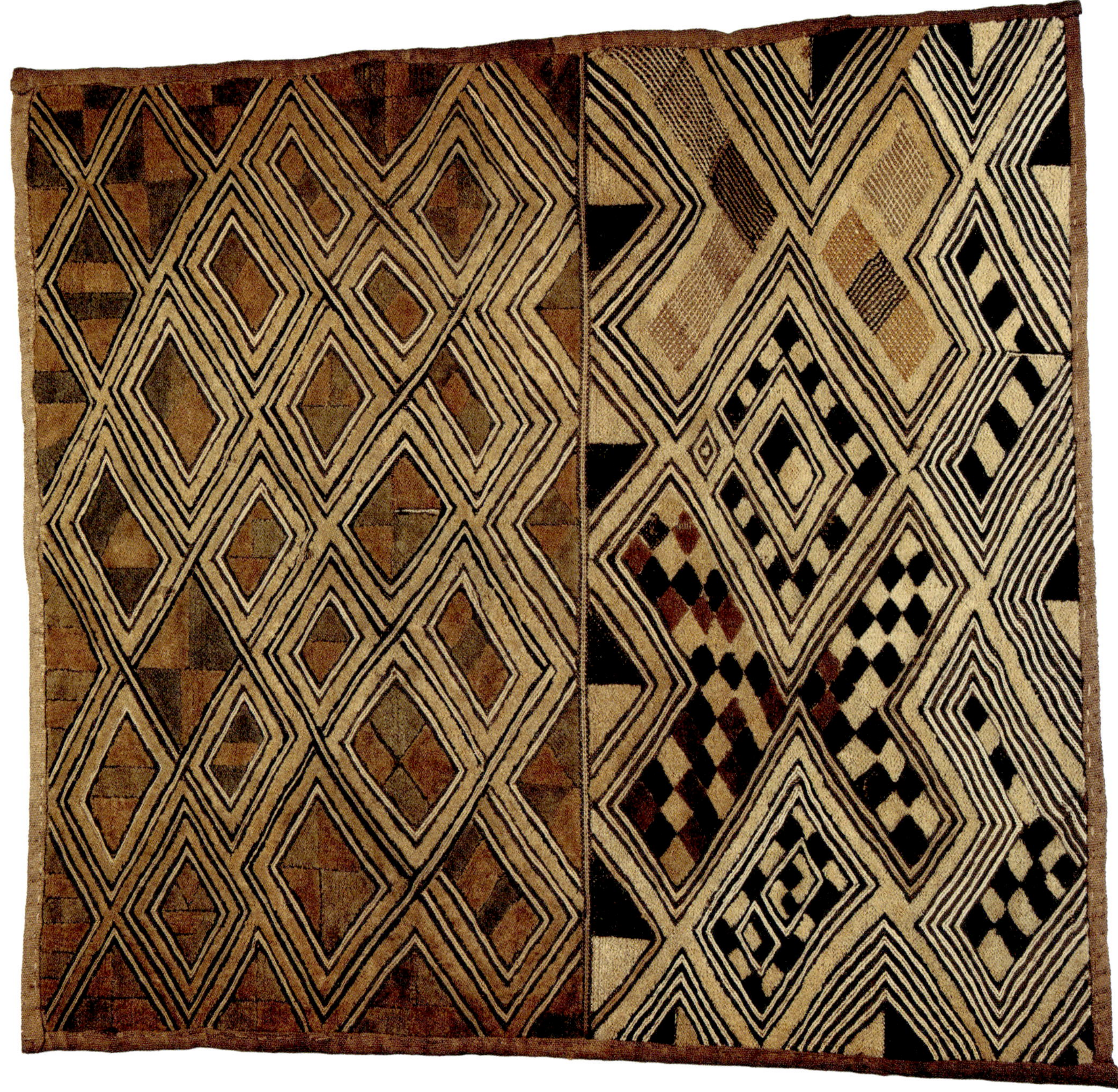

Cat. 10
Prestige Panel, 28¼ × 27½ × 1¼ inches
(71.8 × 69.9 × 3.2 cm). 2020.24.21

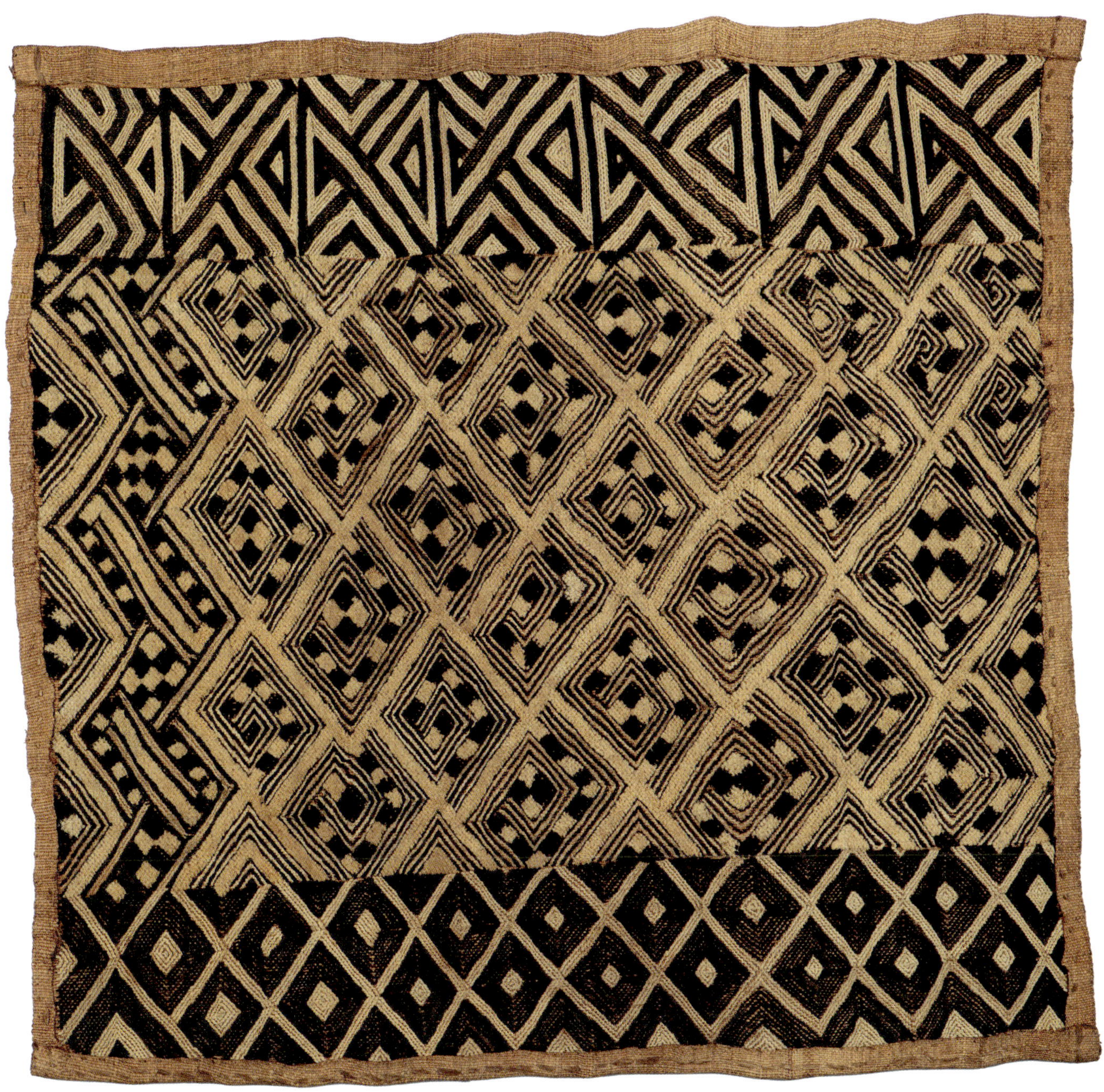

Cat. 11
Prestige Panel, 23½ × 22⅝ × 1¼ inches
(59.7 × 57.5 × 3.2 cm). 2020.24.59

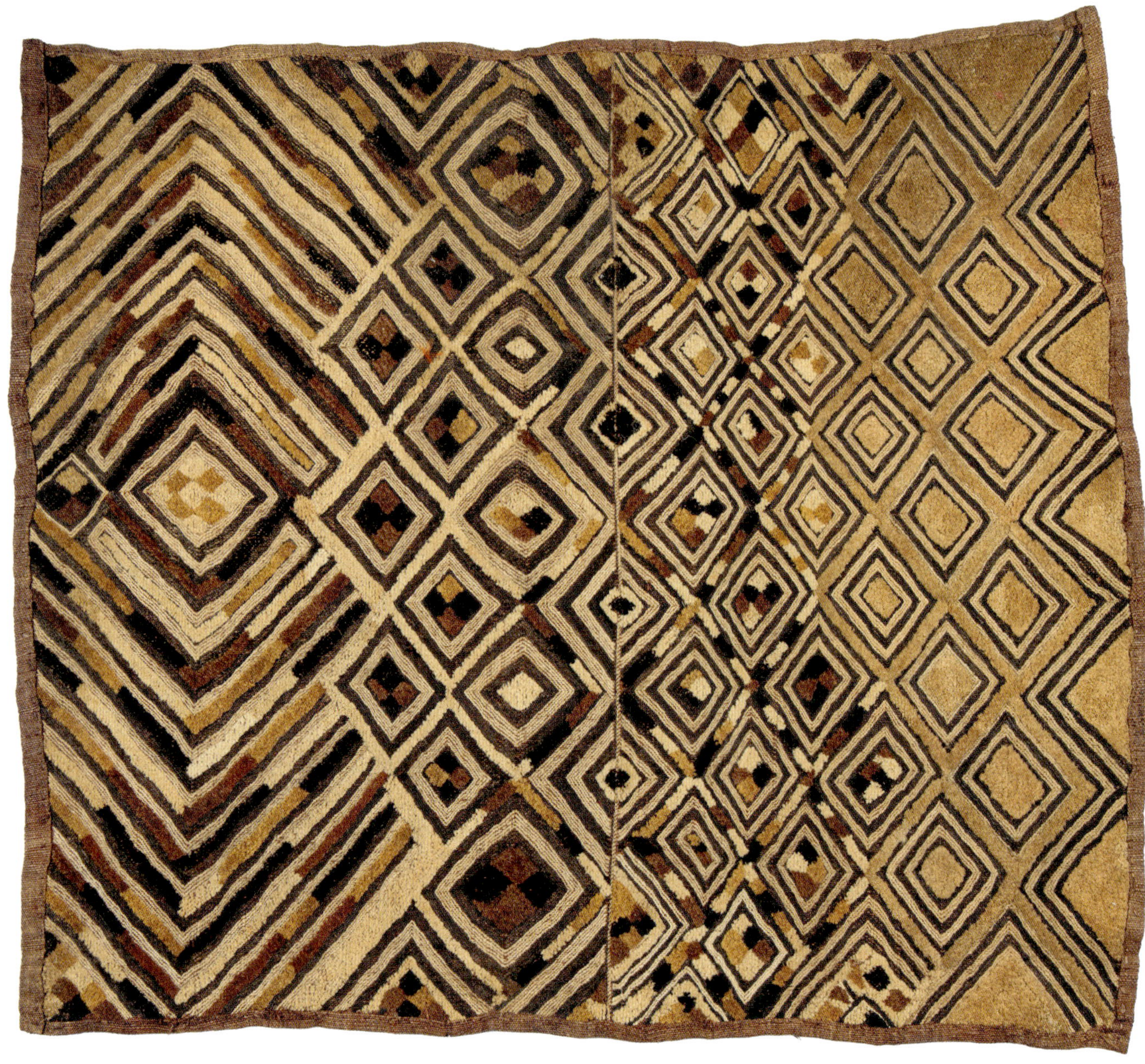

Cat. 12
Prestige Panel, 25¼ × 23⅜ inches
(64.1 × 59.4 cm). 2020.24.26

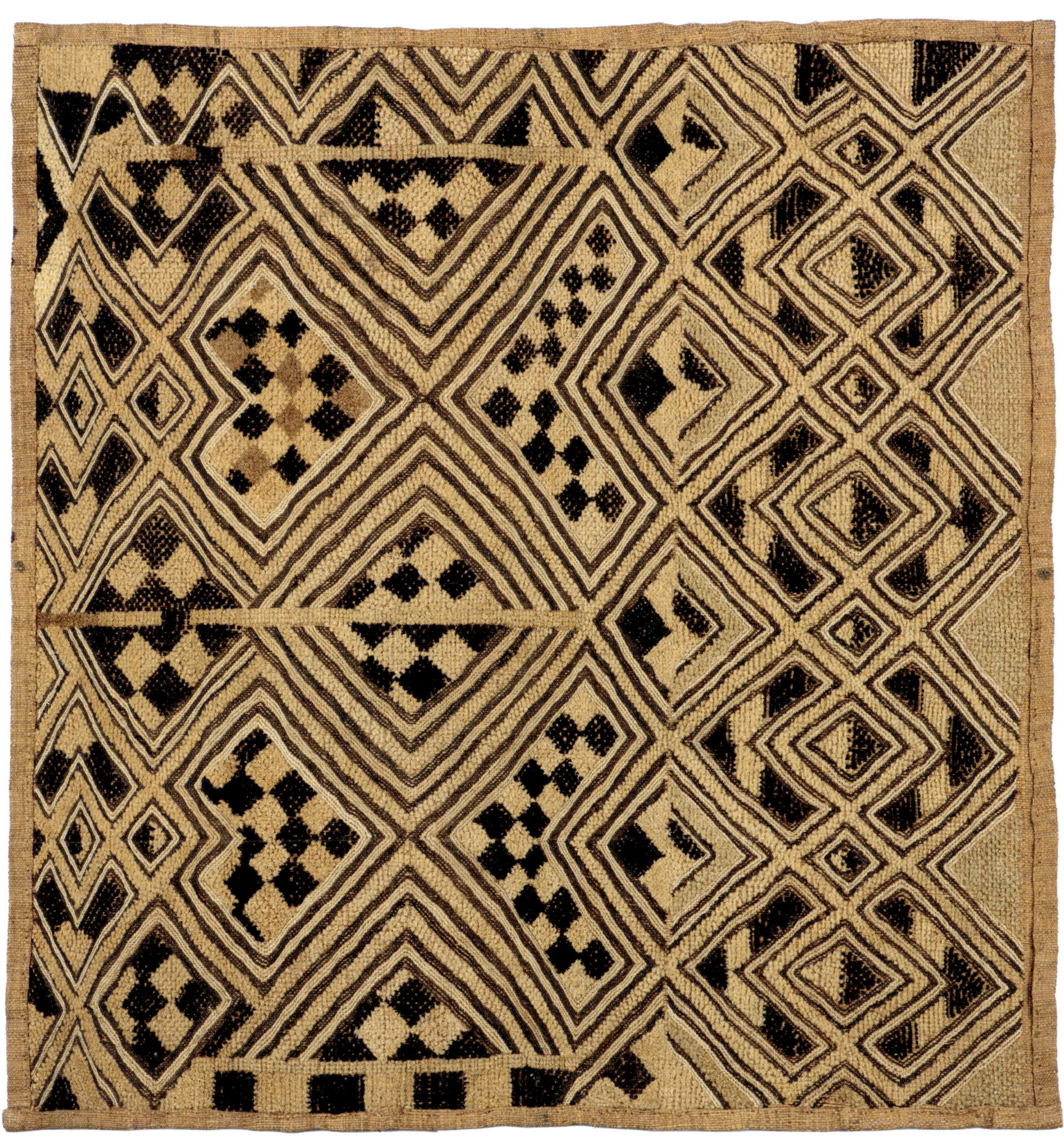

Cat. 13
Prestige Panel, 24⅛ × 23¼ × 1¼ inches
(61.3 × 59 × 3.2 cm). 2020.24.3

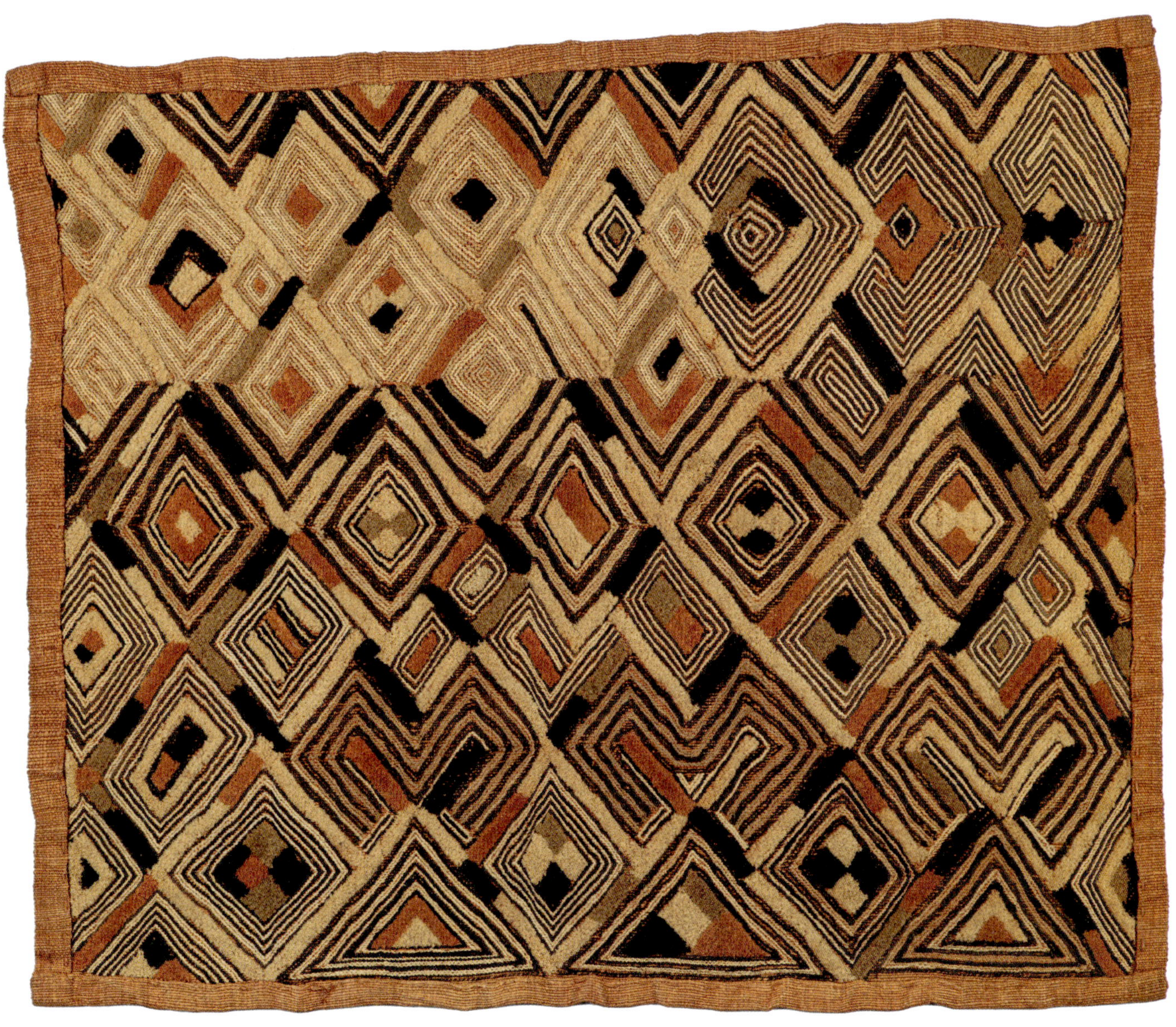

Cat. 14
Prestige Panel, 24⅞ × 21⅜ × 1¼ inches
(63.2 × 54.3 × 3.2 cm). 2020.24.6

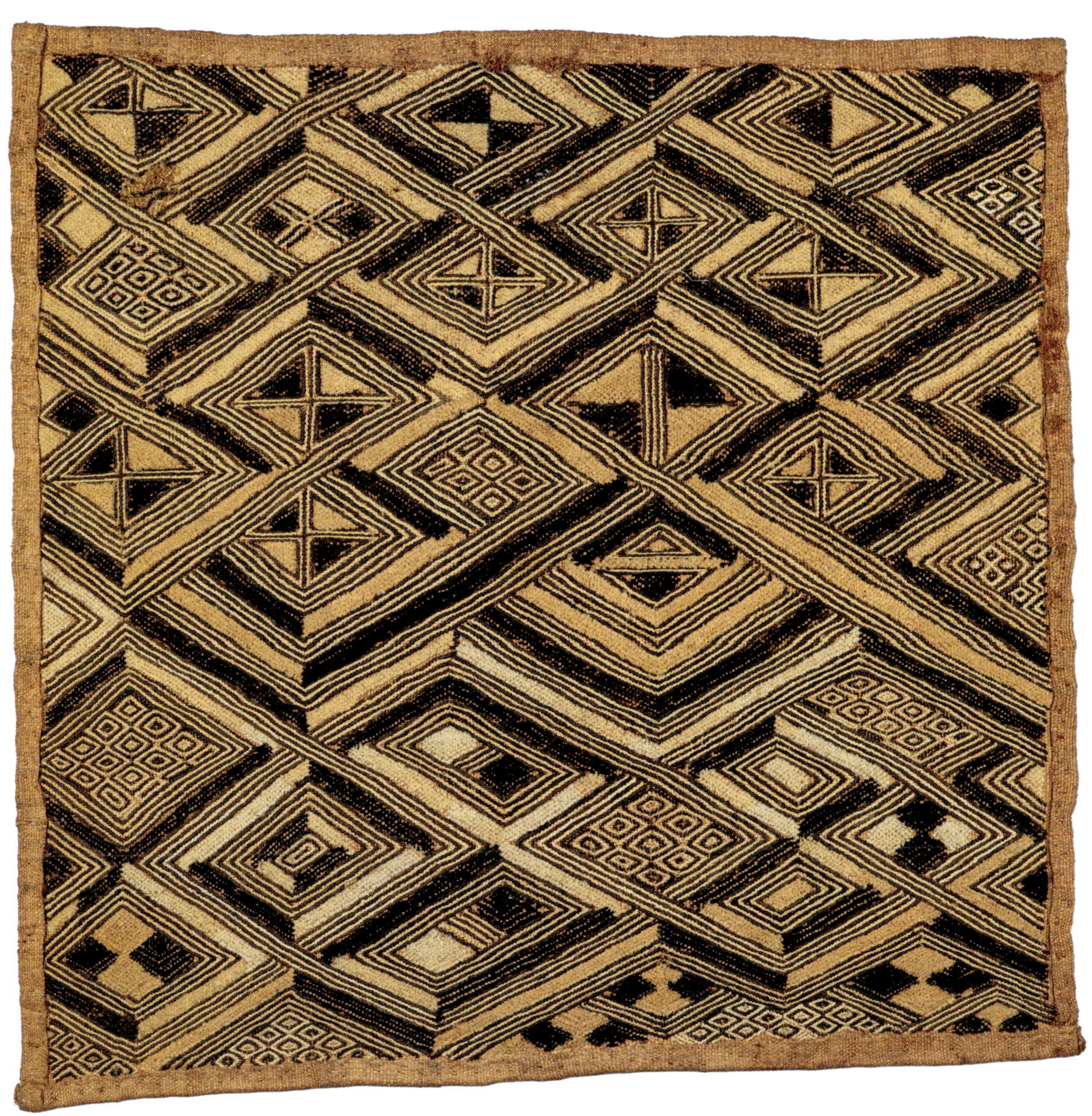

Cat. 15
Prestige Panel, 23½ × 23 × 1¼ inches
(59.7 × 58.4 × 3.2 cm). 2020.24.60

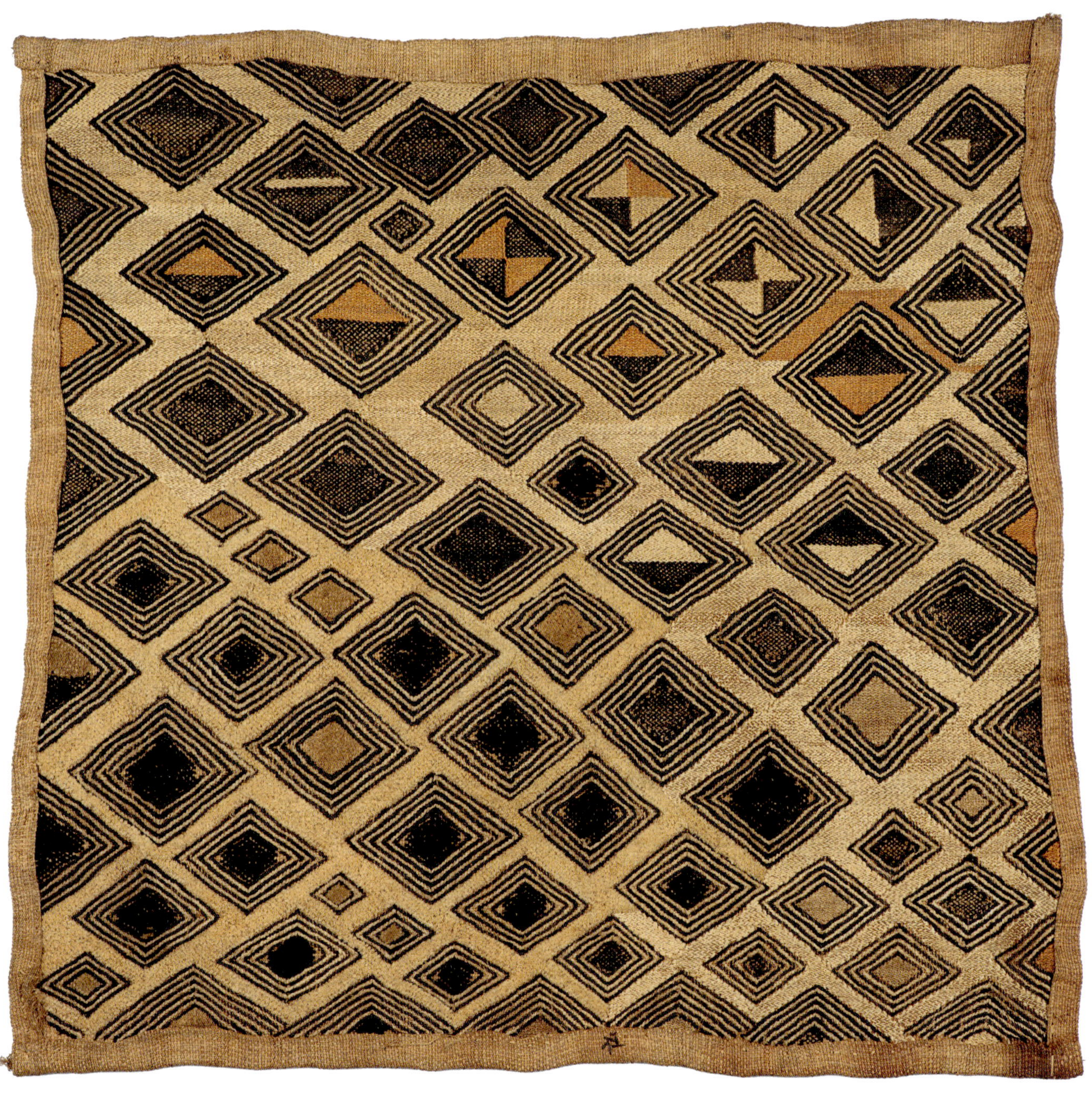

Cat. 16
Prestige Panel, 25¼ × 23⅜ × 1¼ inches
(64.1 × 59.4 × 3.2 cm). 2020.24.55

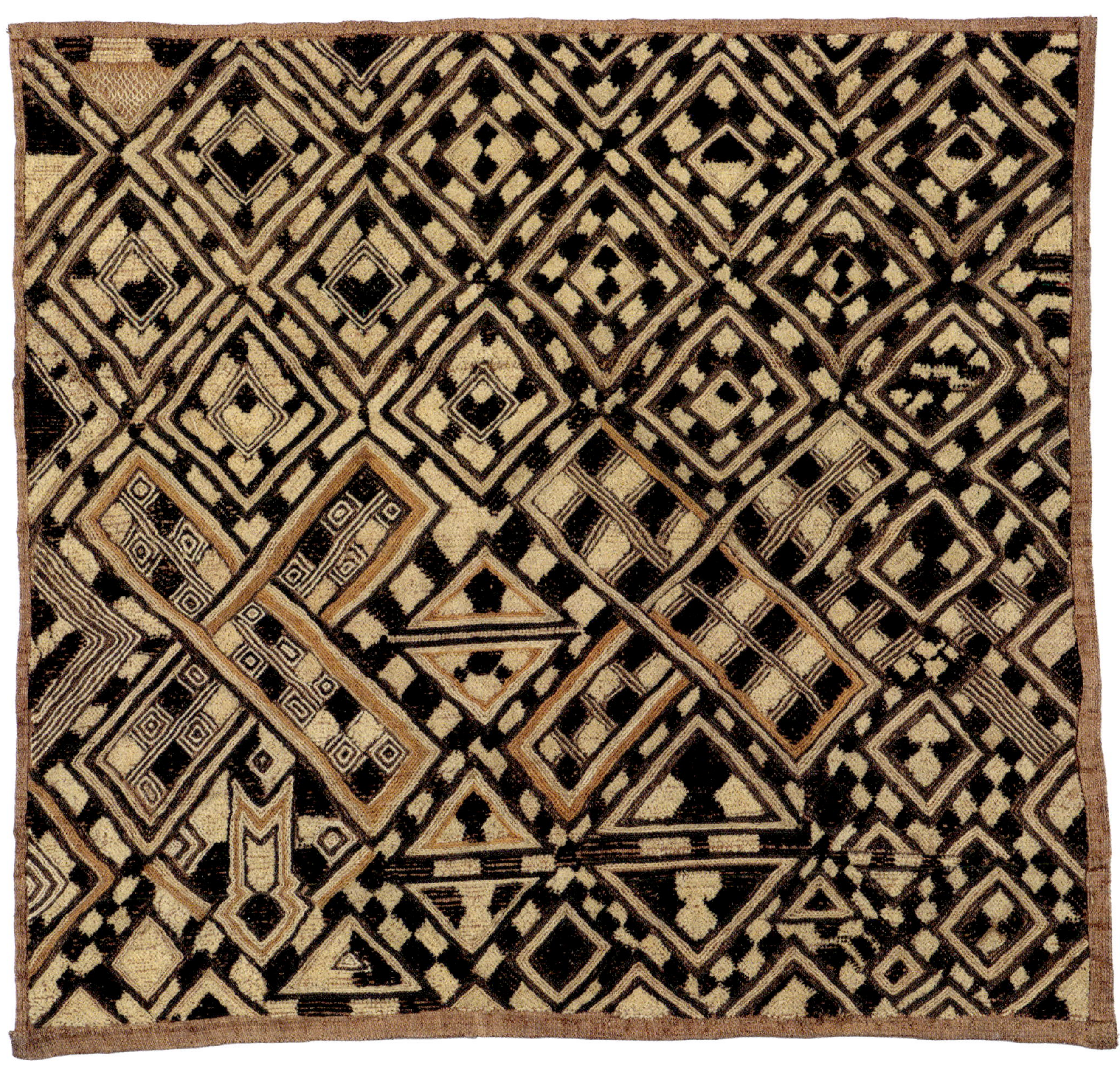

Cat. 17
Prestige Panel, 24½ × 23⅞ × 1¼ inches
(62.2 × 60.6 × 3.2 cm). 2020.24.58

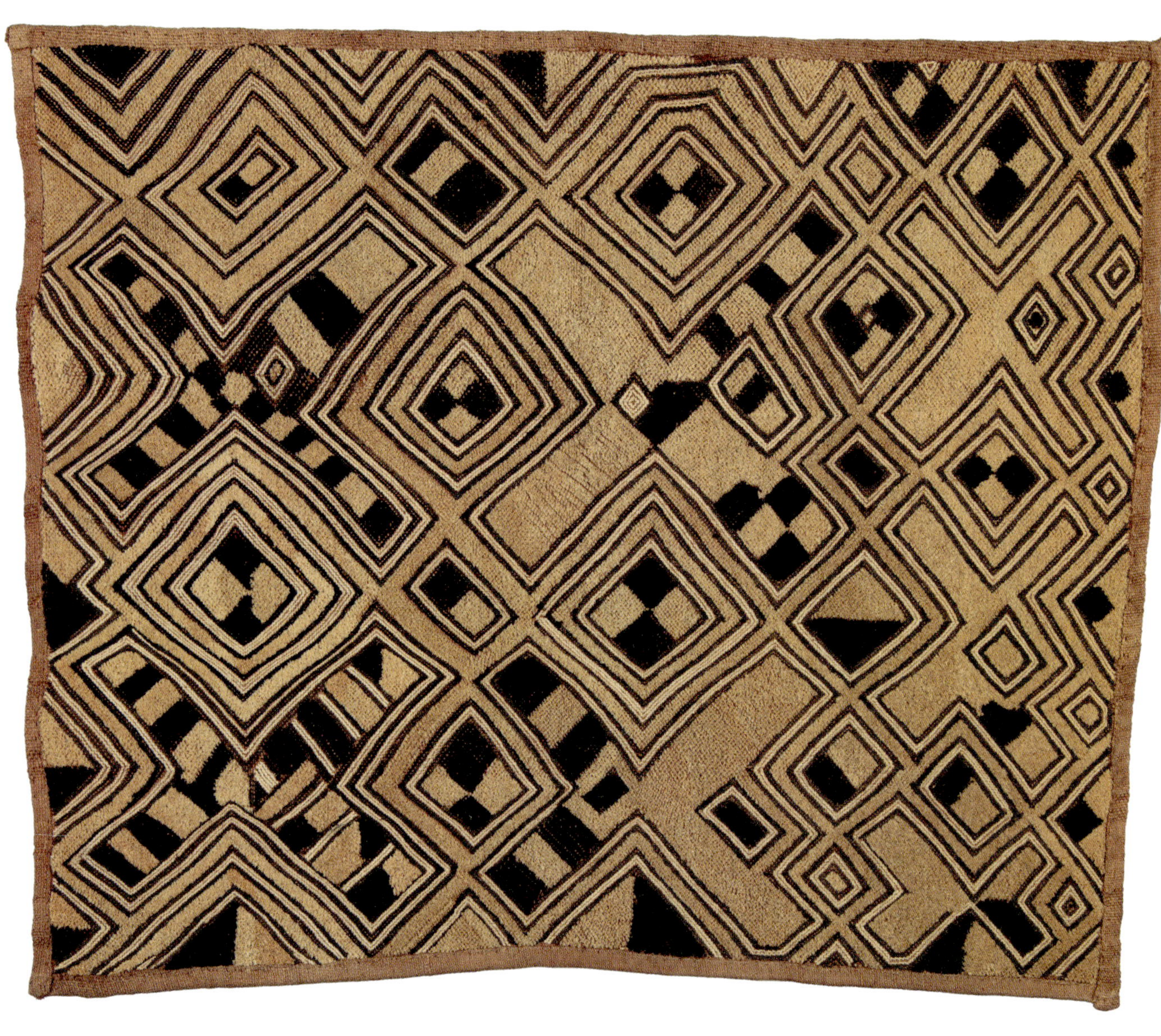

Cat. 18
Prestige Panel, 23¾ × 27¾ × 1¼ inches
(60.3 × 70.5 × 3.2 cm). 2020.24.4

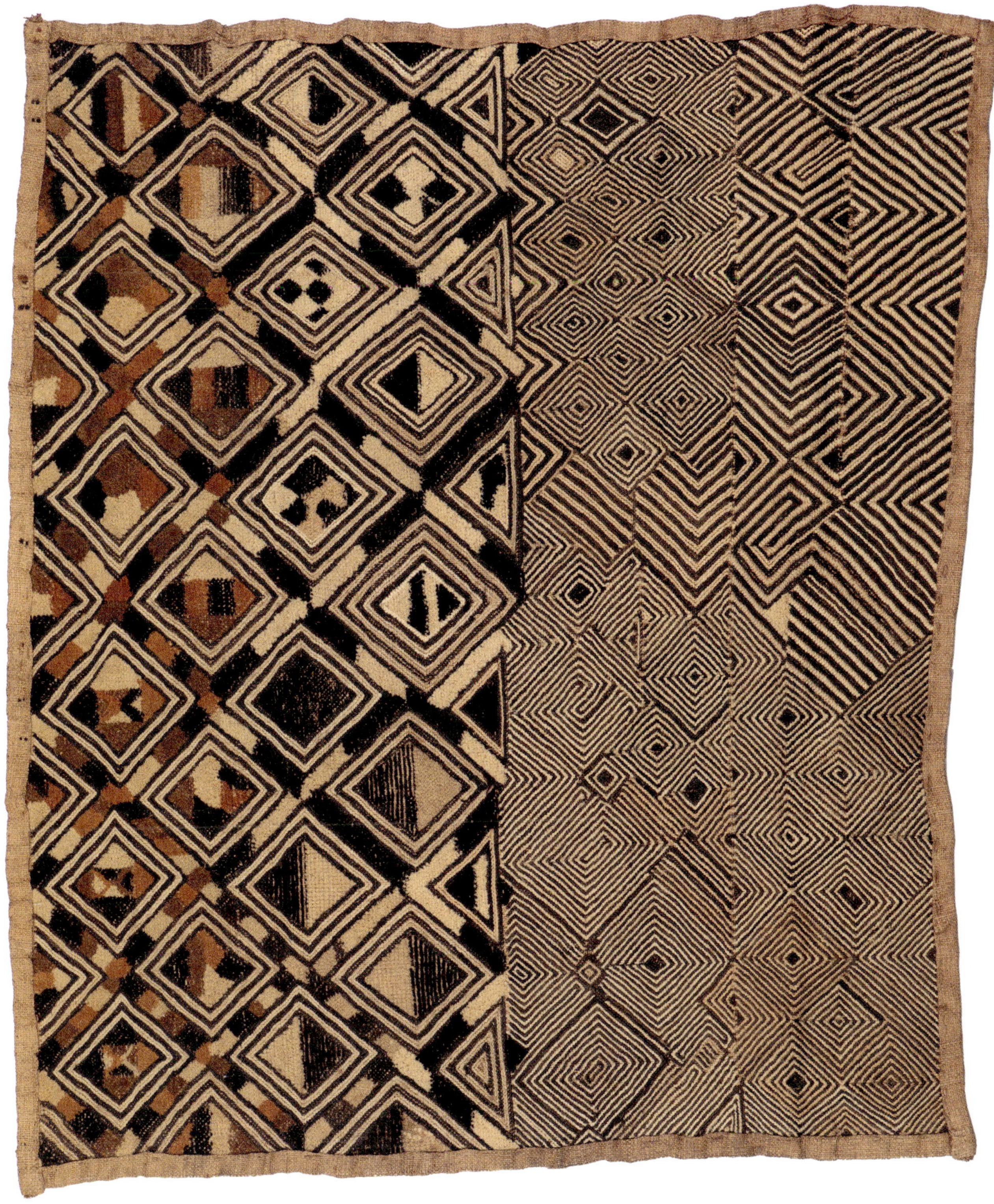

Cat. 19
Prestige Panel, 27 × 23 × 1¼ inches
(68.6 × 58.4 × 3.2 cm) (framed). 2020.24.15

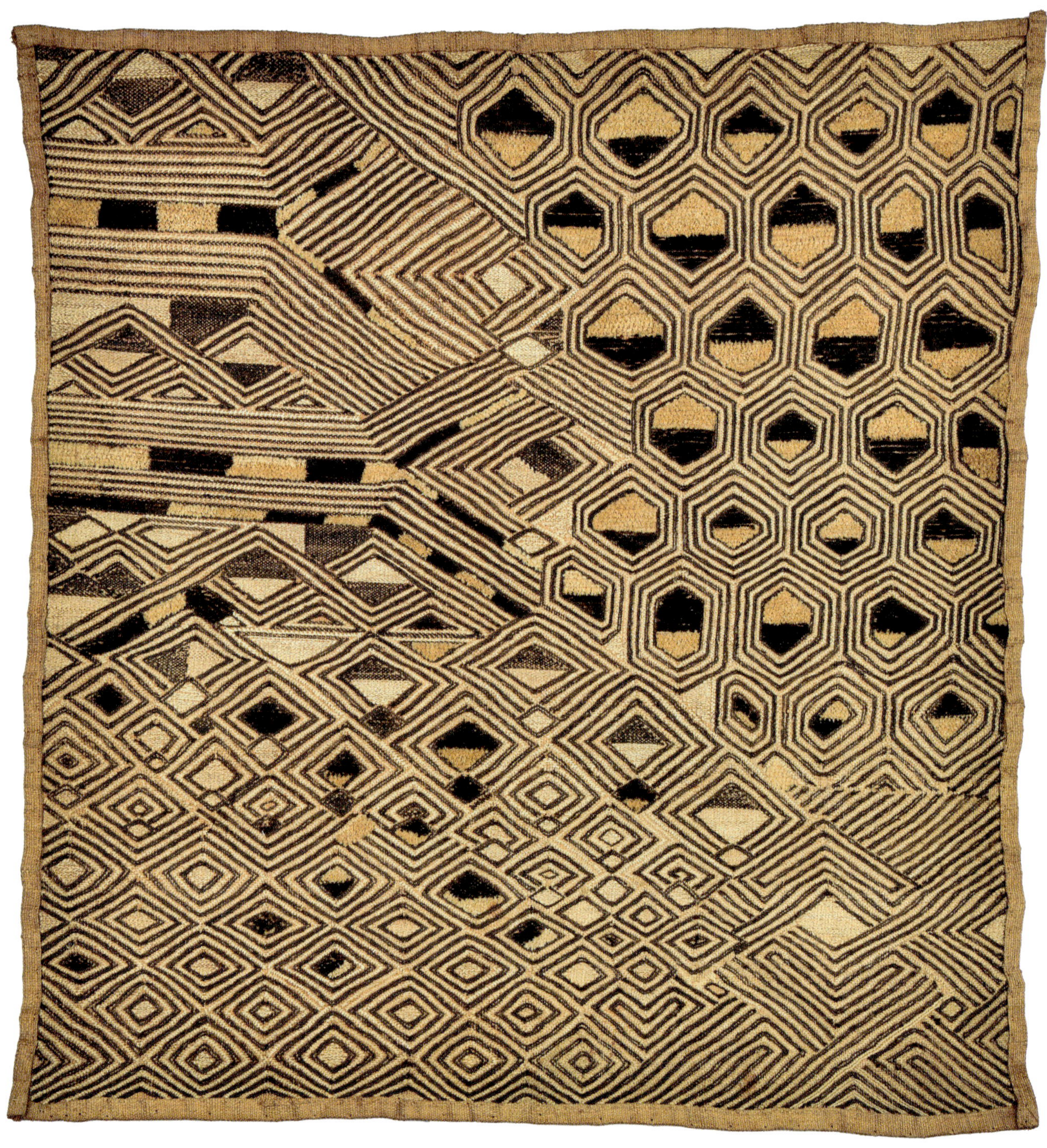

Cat. 20
Prestige Panel, 27⅞ × 27⅛ × 1¼ inches
(70.8 × 68.9 × 3.2 cm) (framed). 2020.24.24

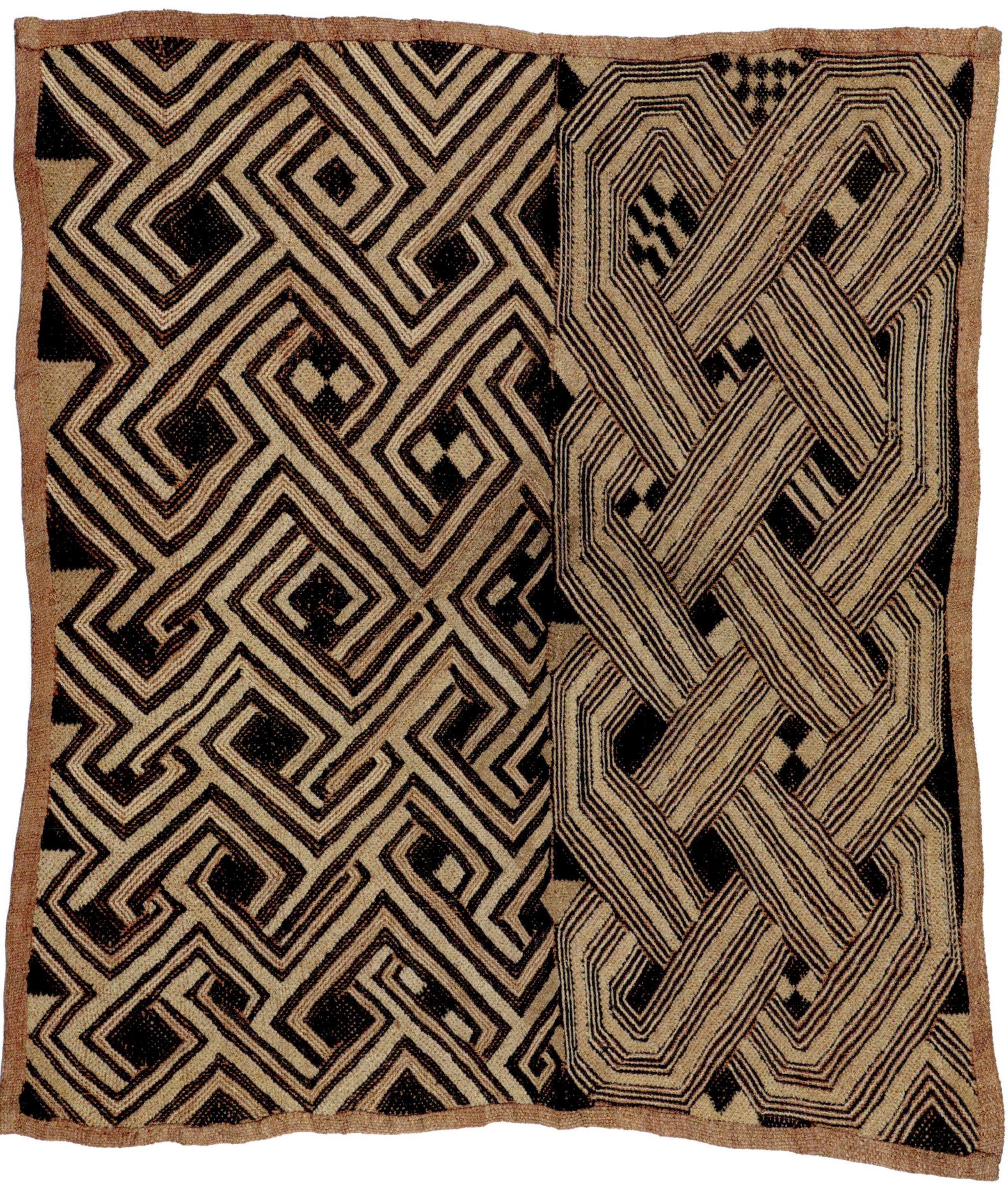

Cat. 21
Prestige Panel, 22 × 19⅞ inches
(55.9 × 50.5 cm). 2020.24.36

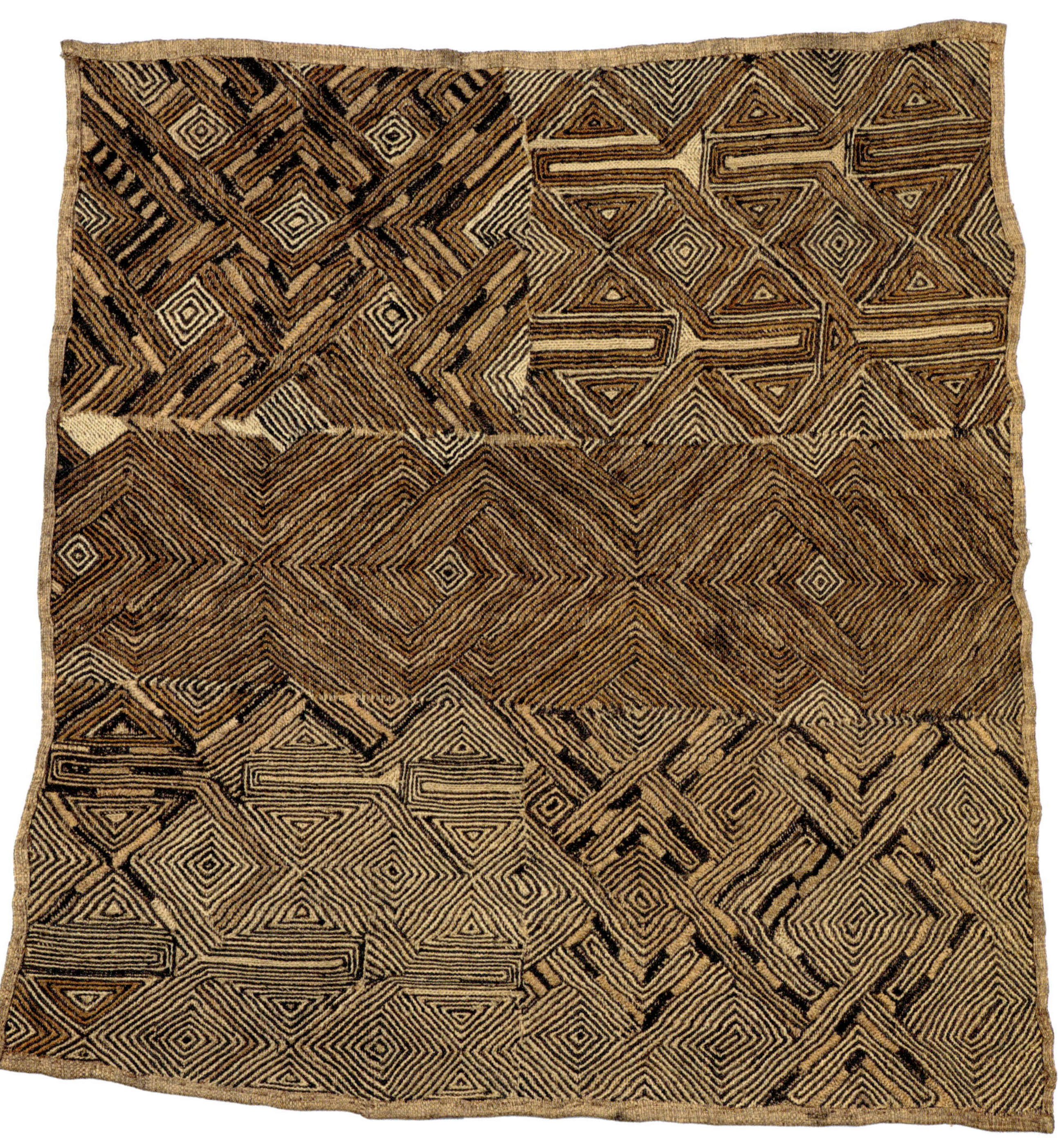

Cat. 22
Prestige Panel, 19¾ × 19⅜ inches
(50.2 × 49.2 cm). 2020.24.39

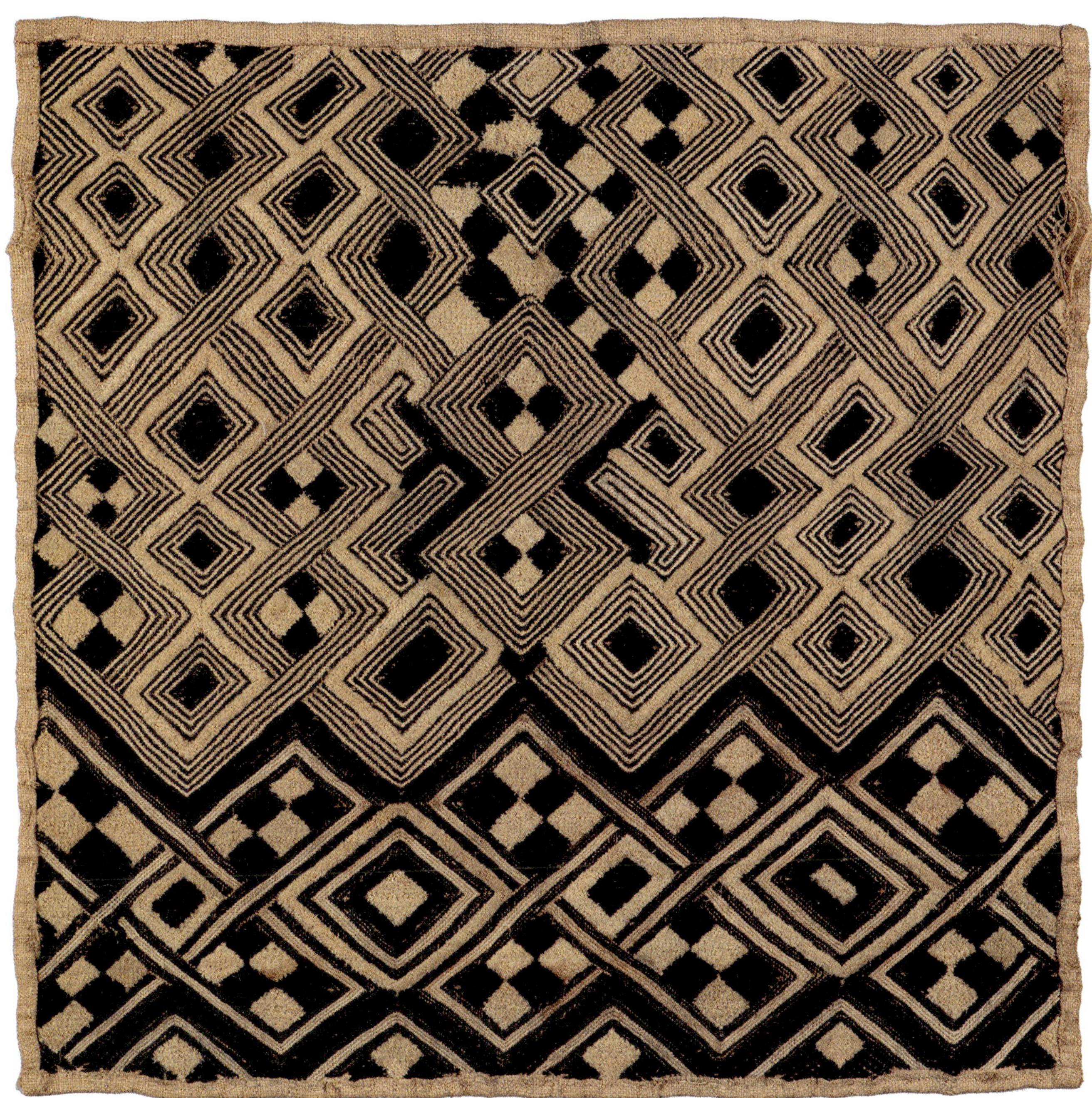

Cat. 23
Prestige Panel, 22⅝ × 23⅛ × 1¼ inches
(57.5 × 58.7 × 3.2 cm) (framed). 2020.24.1

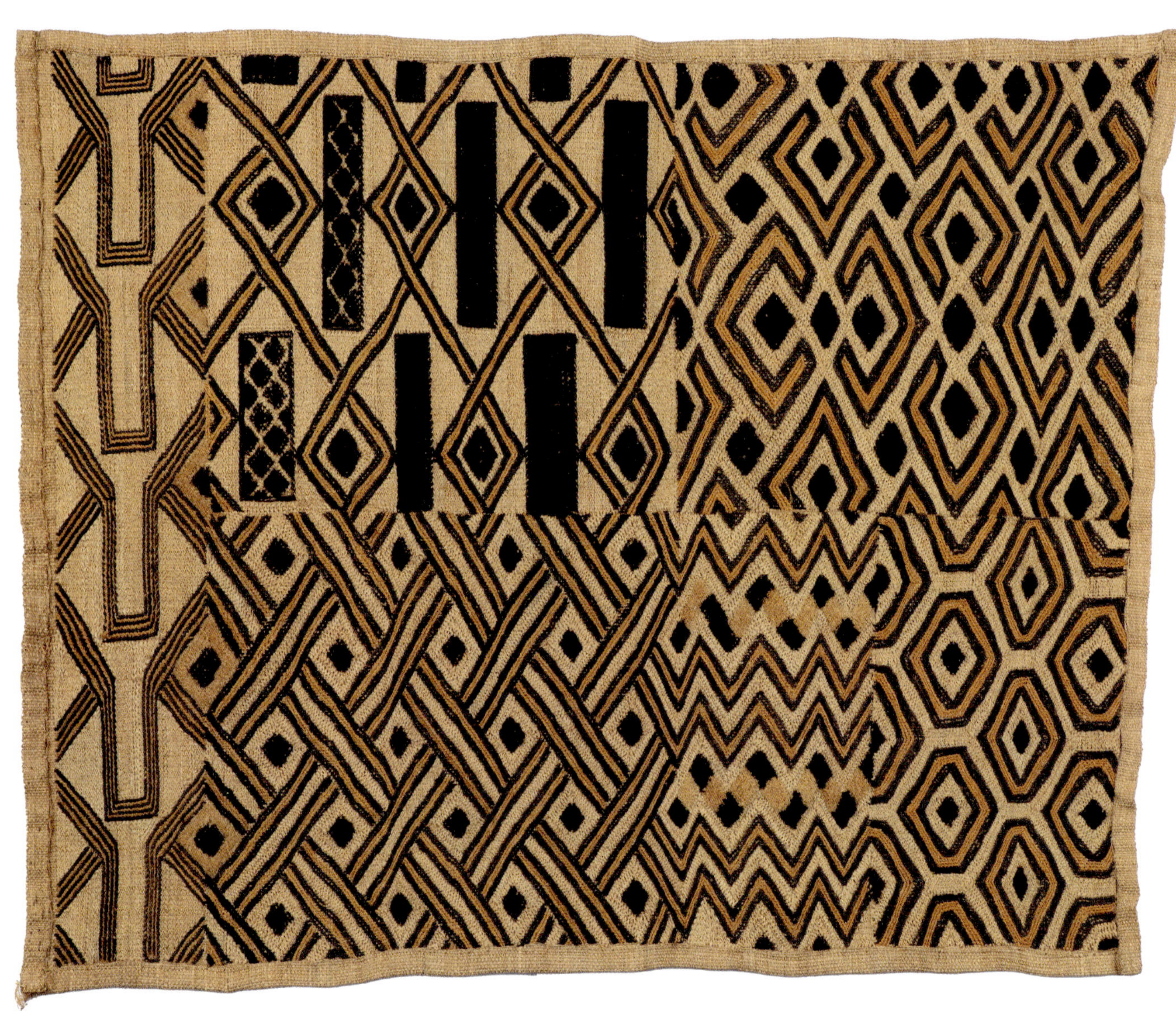

Cat. 24
Prestige Panel, 26⅞ × 22¾ × 1¼ inches
(68.3 × 57.8 × 3.2 cm) (framed). 2020.24.7

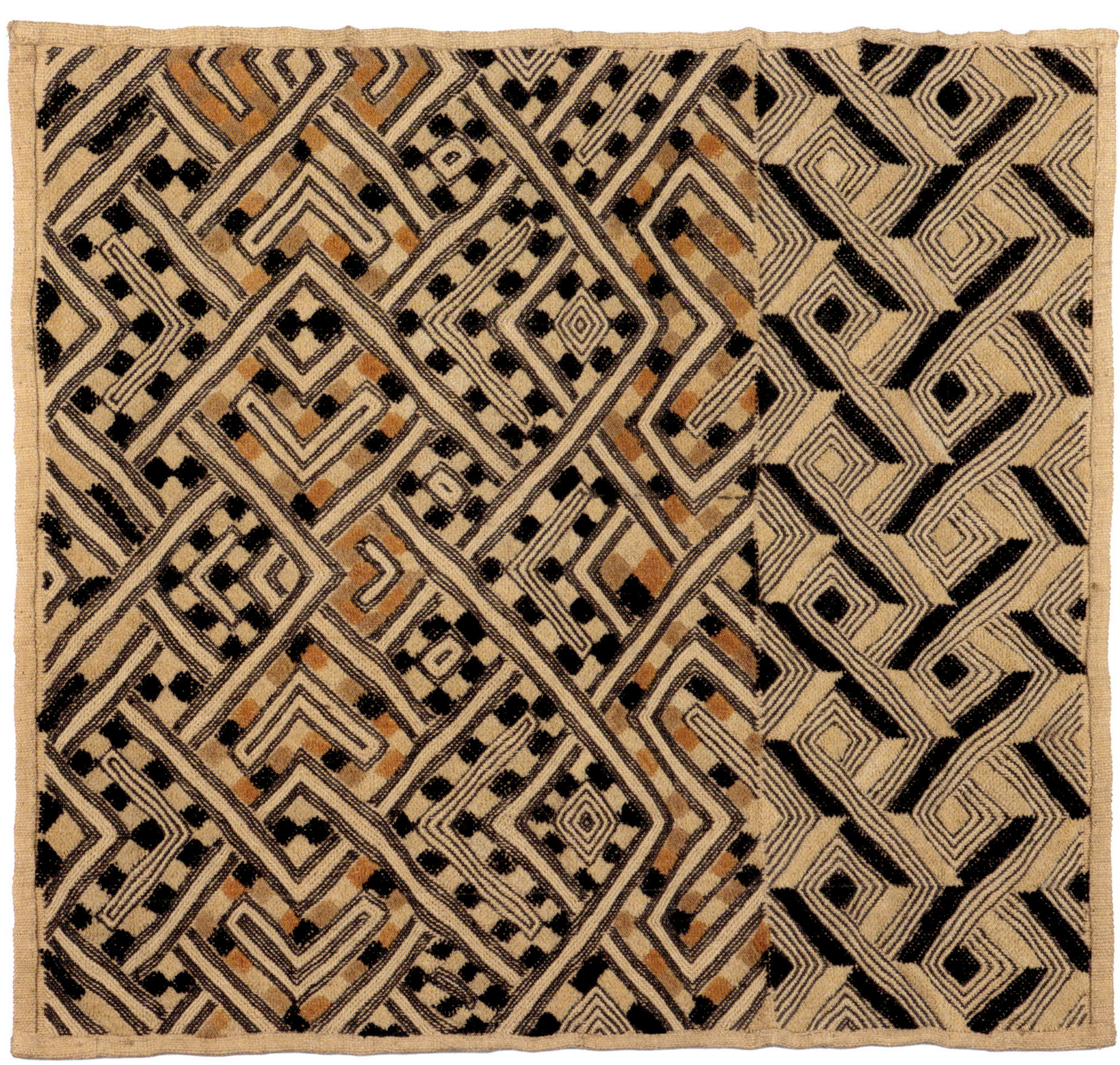

Cat. 25
Prestige Panel, 26⅛ × 23½ × 1¼ inches
(66.4 × 59.7 × 3.2 cm) (framed). 2020.24.12

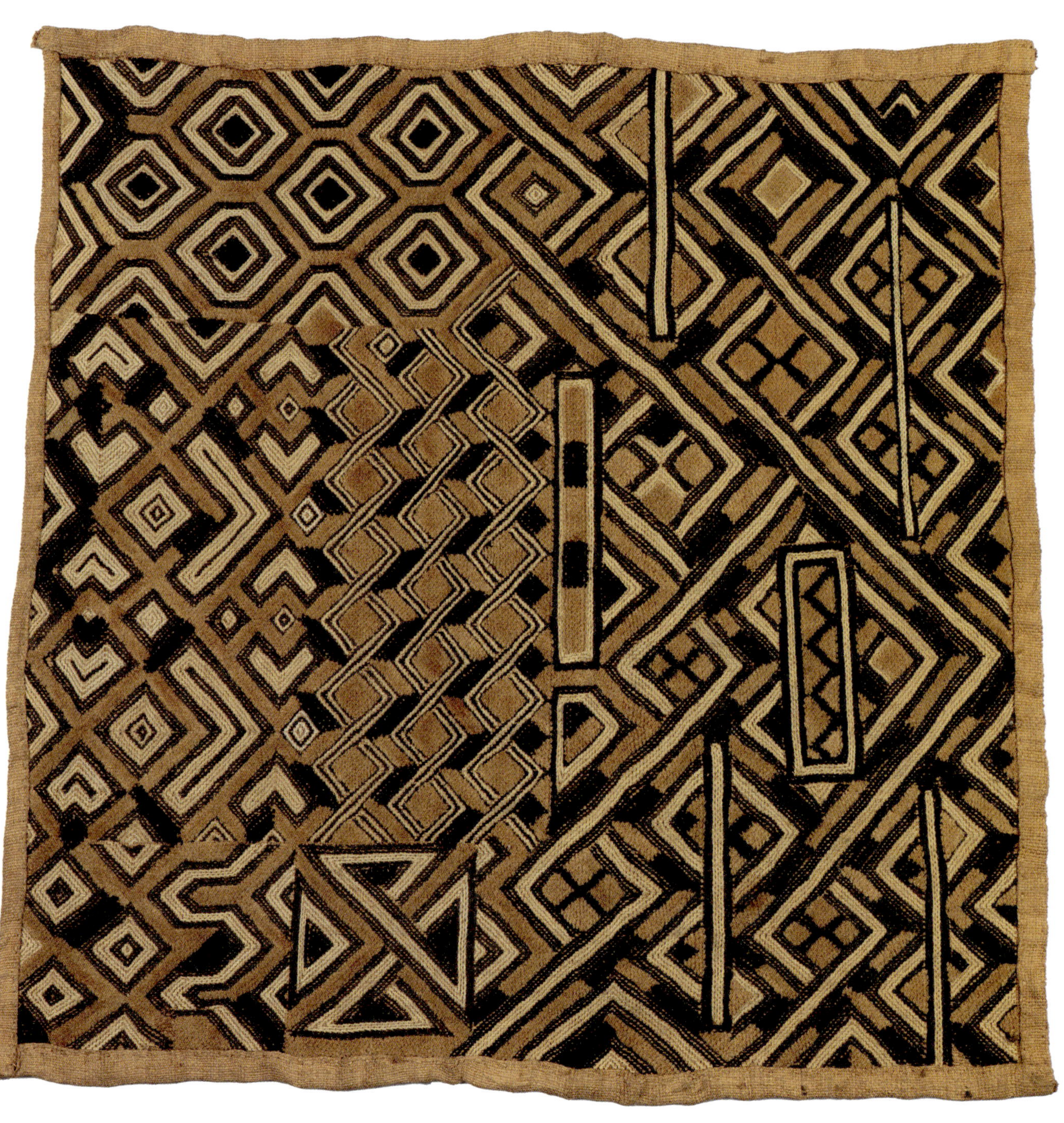

Cat. 26
Prestige Panel, 23⅜ × 23⅜ × 1¼ inches
(59.4 × 59.4 × 3.2 cm) (framed). 2020.24.19

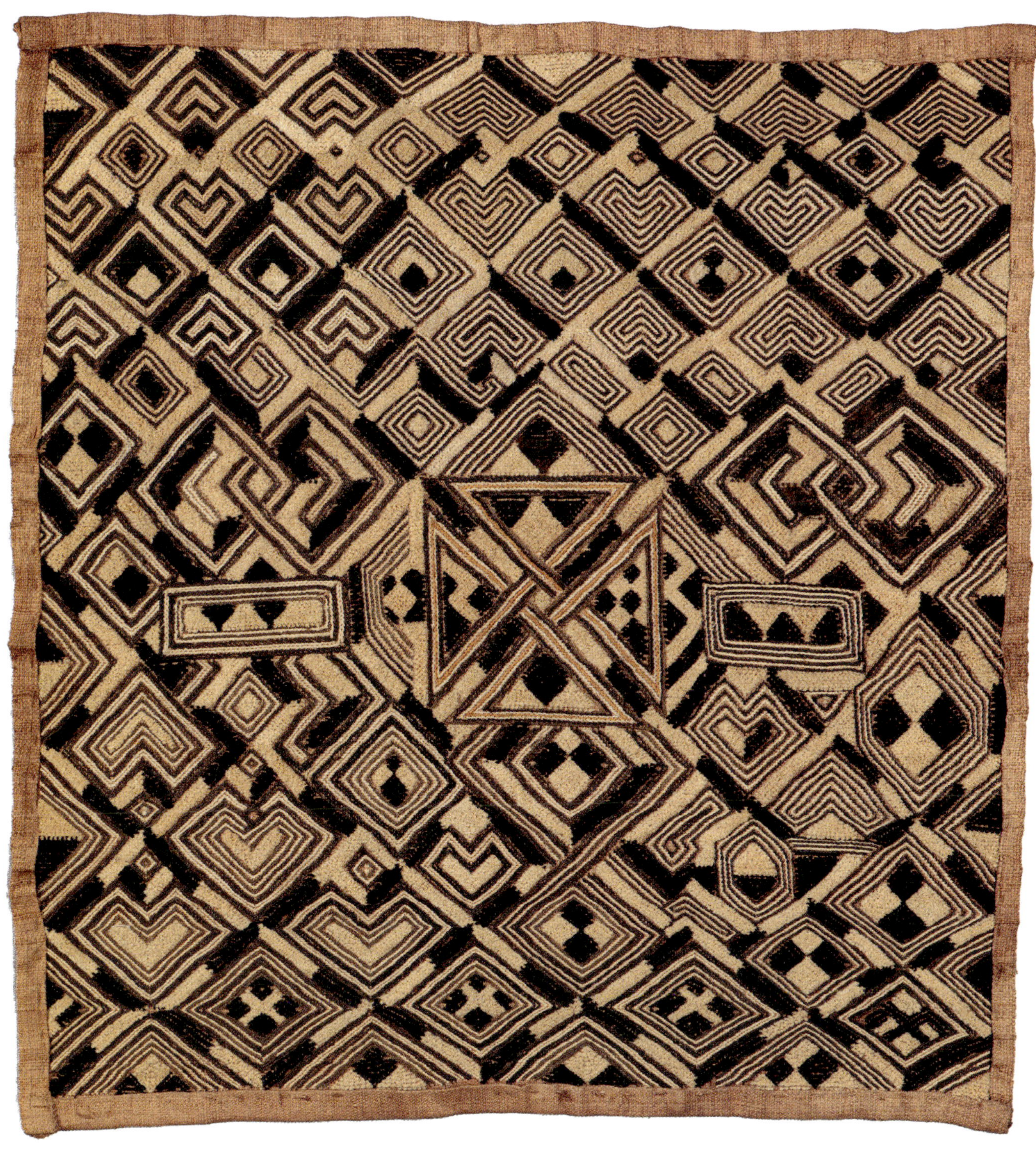

Cat. 27
Prestige Panel, 24⅛ × 23 × 1¼ inches
(61.3 × 58.4 × 3.2 cm) (framed). 2020.24.2

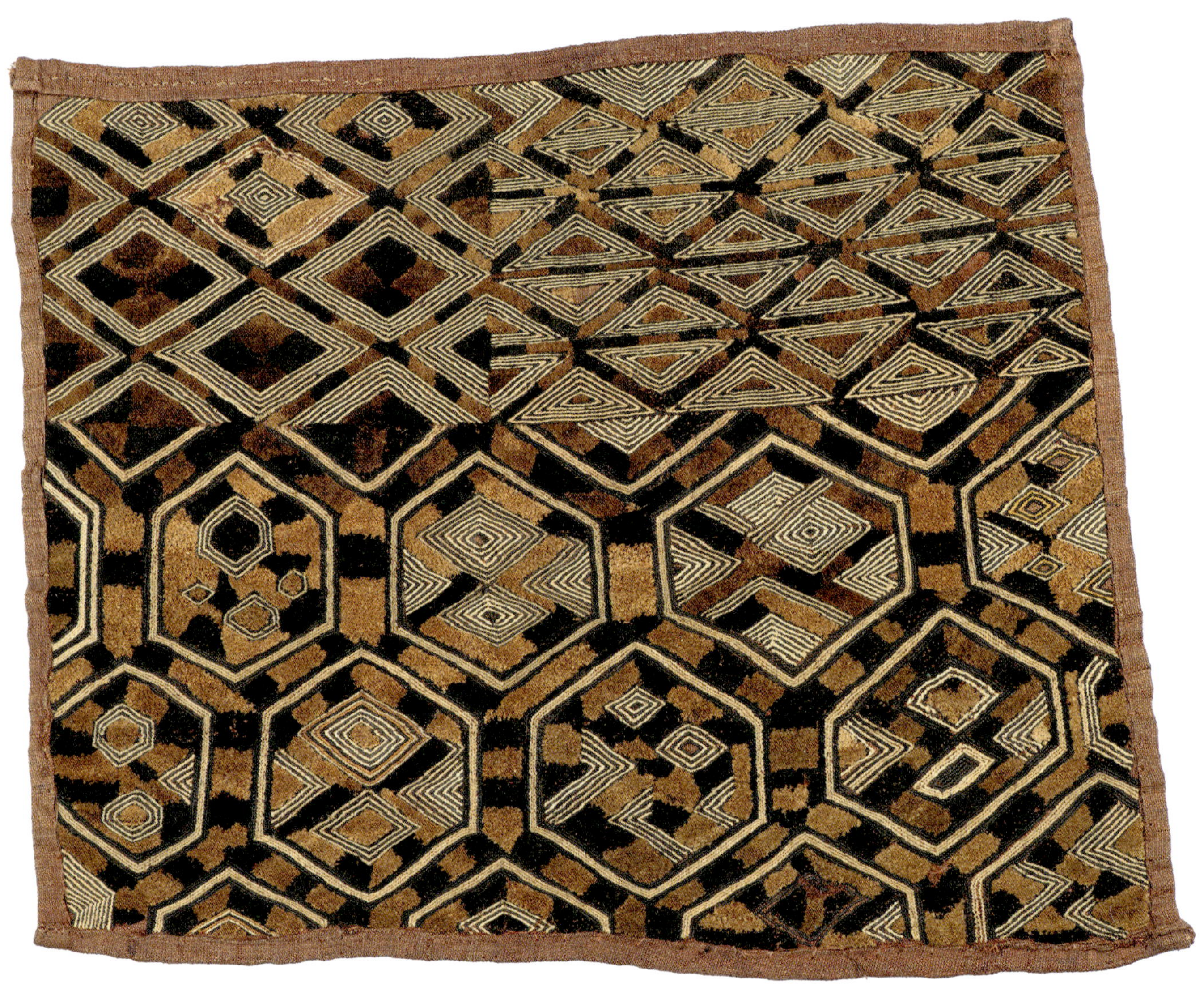

Cat. 28
Prestige Panel, 19½ × 15¾ inches
(49.5 × 40 cm). 2020.24.41

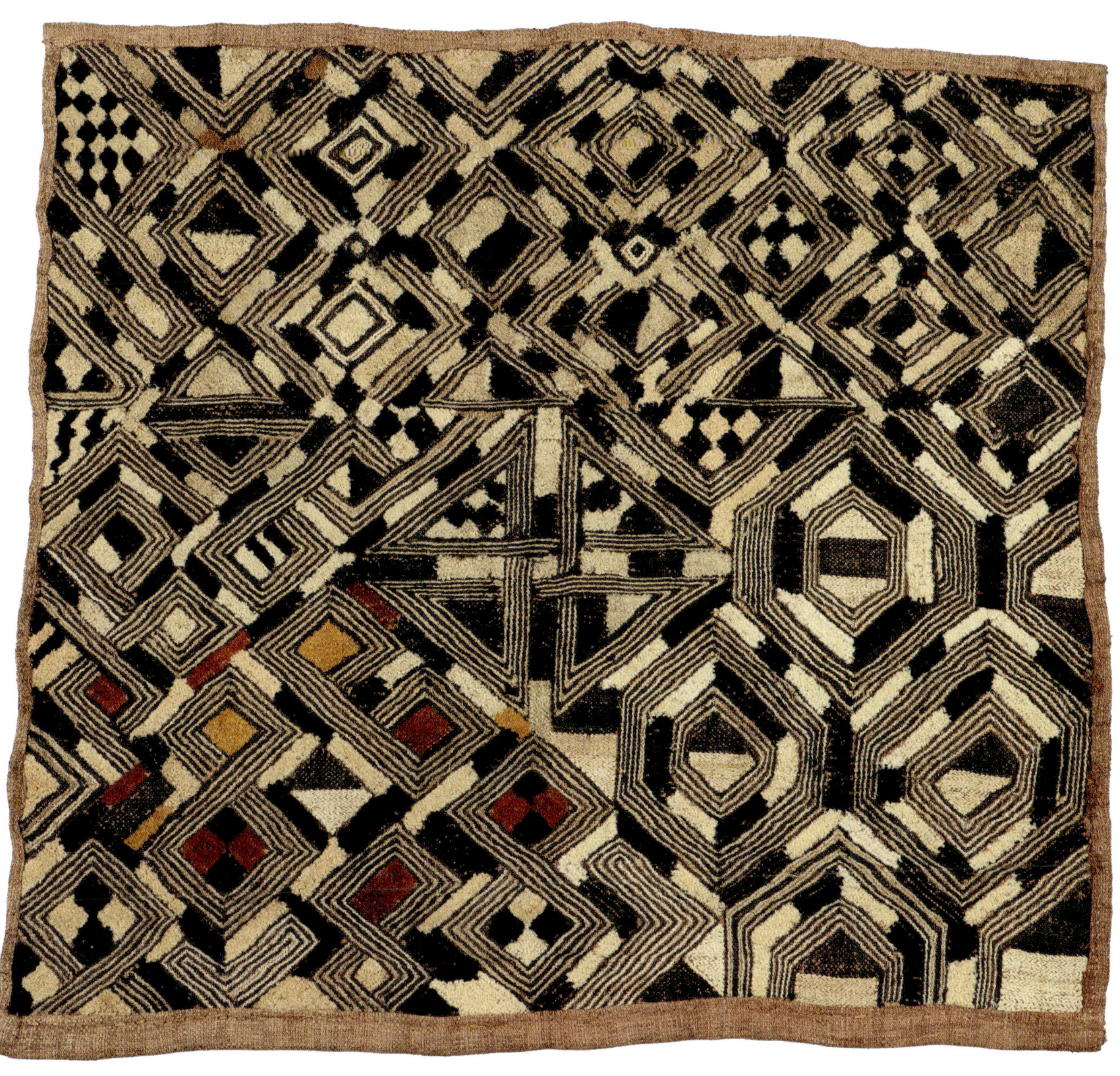

Cat. 29
Prestige Panel, 21¼ × 18½ inches
(54 × 47 cm). 2020.24.34

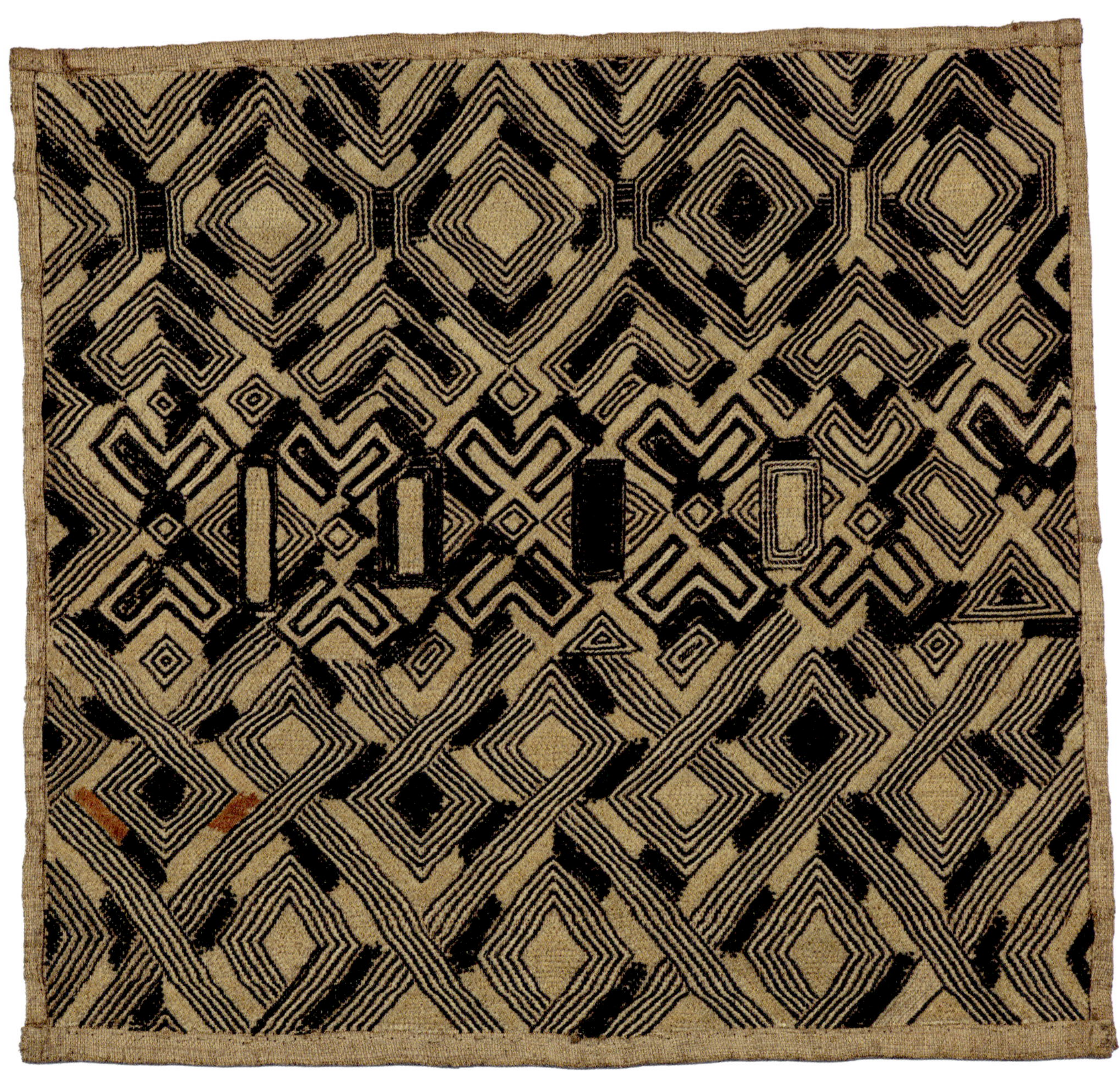

Cat. 30
Prestige Panel, 23⅜ × 22⅛ × 1¼ inches
(59.4 × 56.2 × 3.2 cm) (framed). 2020.24.18

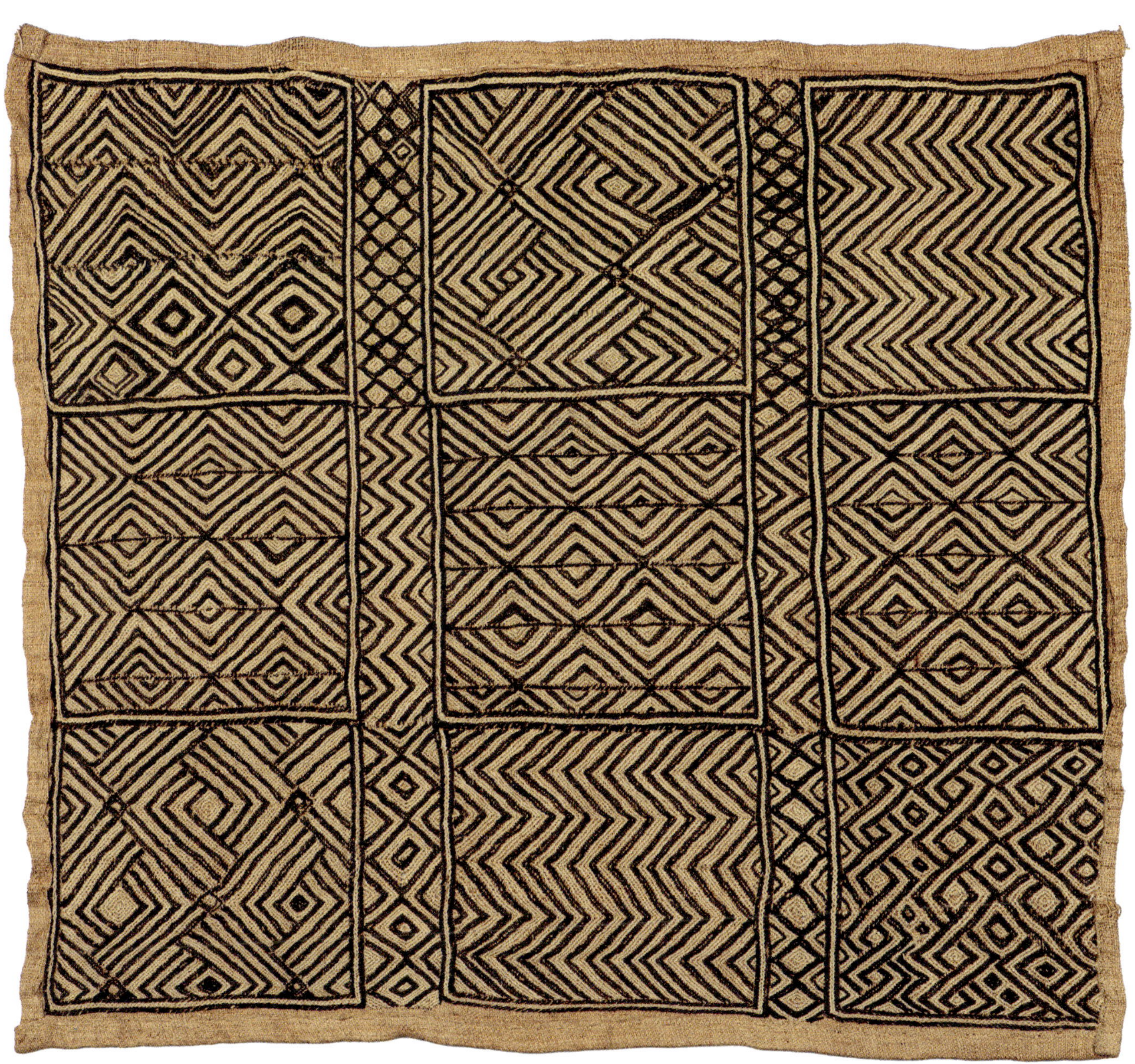

Cat. 31
Prestige Panel, raffia palm fiber, natural dyes;
stem stitch embroidery, 28⅝ × 25⅝ × 1¼ inches
(72.8 × 65.1 × 3.2 cm) (framed). 2020.24.20

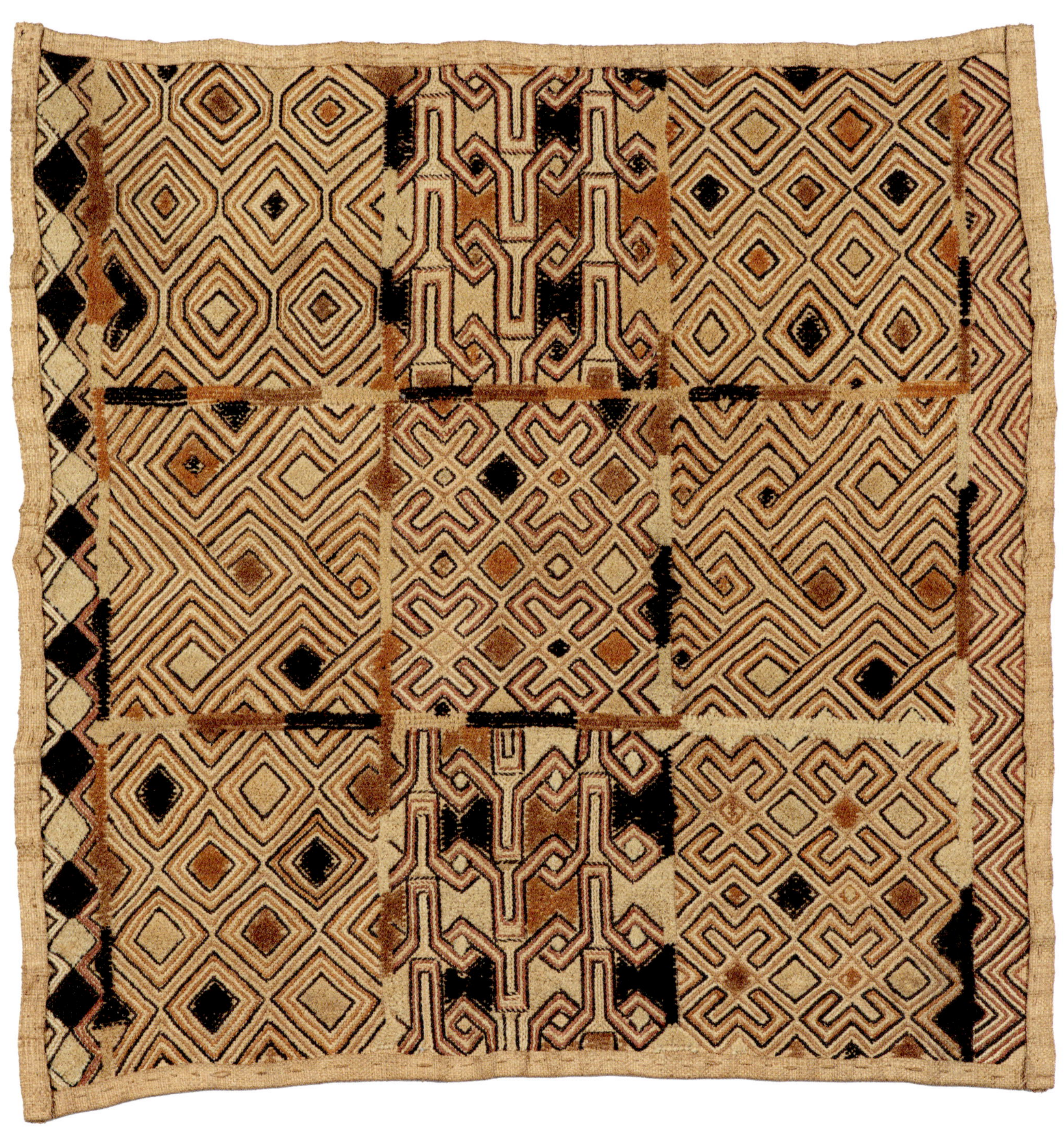

Cat. 32
Prestige Panel, 24¾ × 24⅝ × 1¼ inches
(62.9 × 62.6 × 3.2 cm) (framed). 2020.24.22

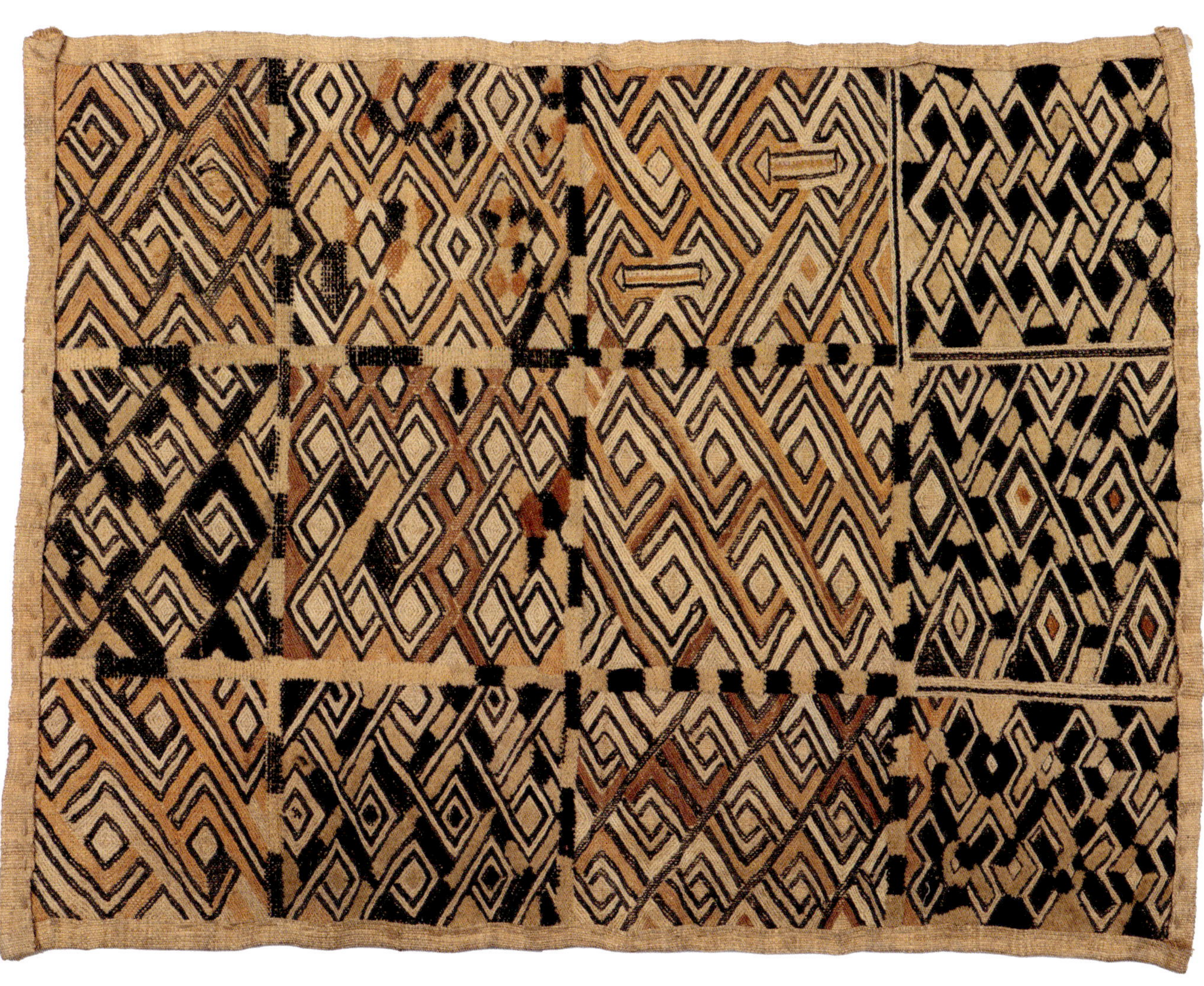

Cat. 33
Prestige Panel, 27 × 21⅛ × 1¼ inches
(68.6 × 53.7 × 3.2 cm) (framed). 2020.24.13

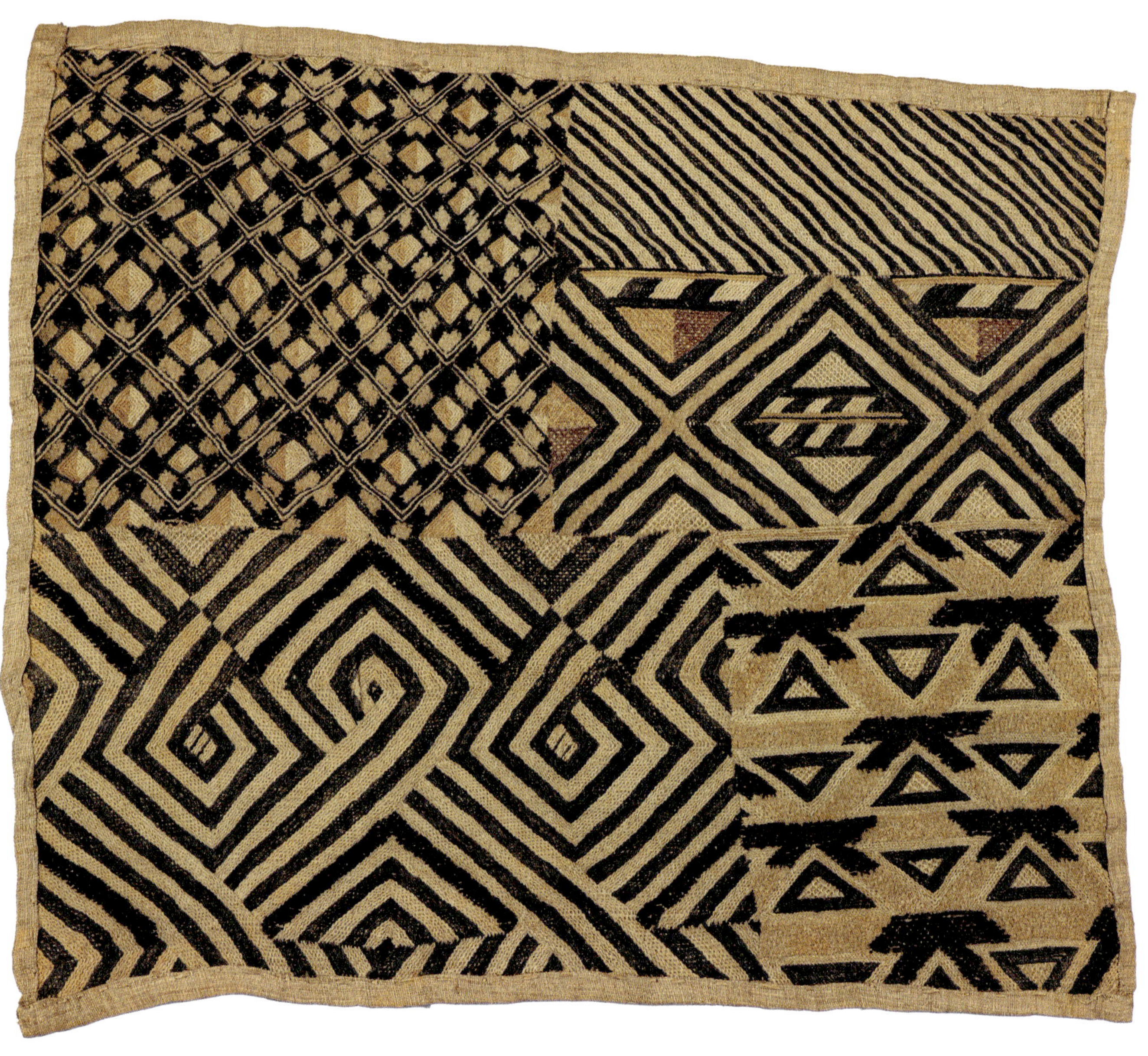

Cat. 34
Prestige Panel, 21½ × 19⅛ inches
(54.6 × 48.6 cm). 2020.24.37

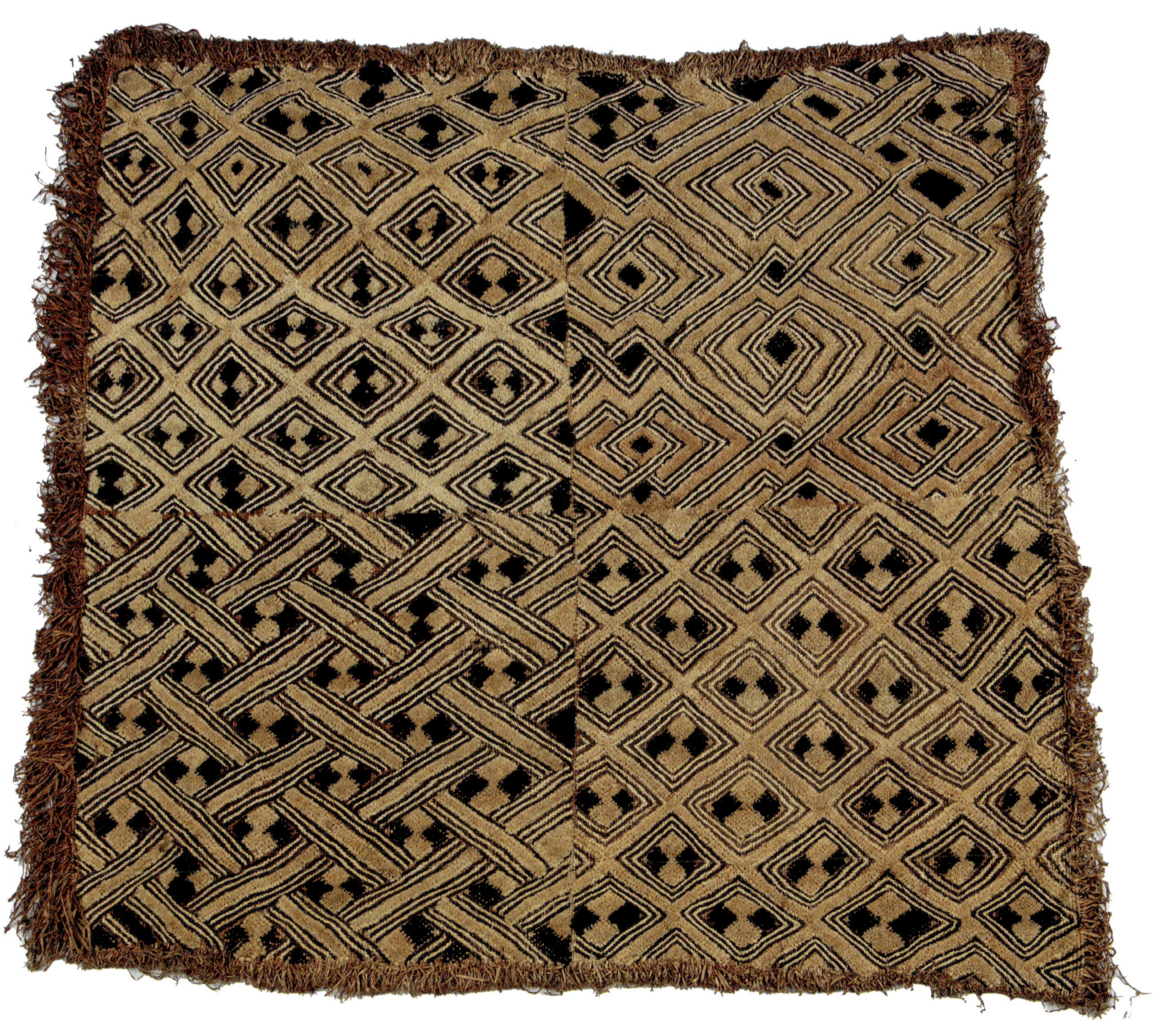

Cat. 35
Prestige Panel, 29½ × 25¾ inches
(74.9 × 65.4 cm). 2020.24.27

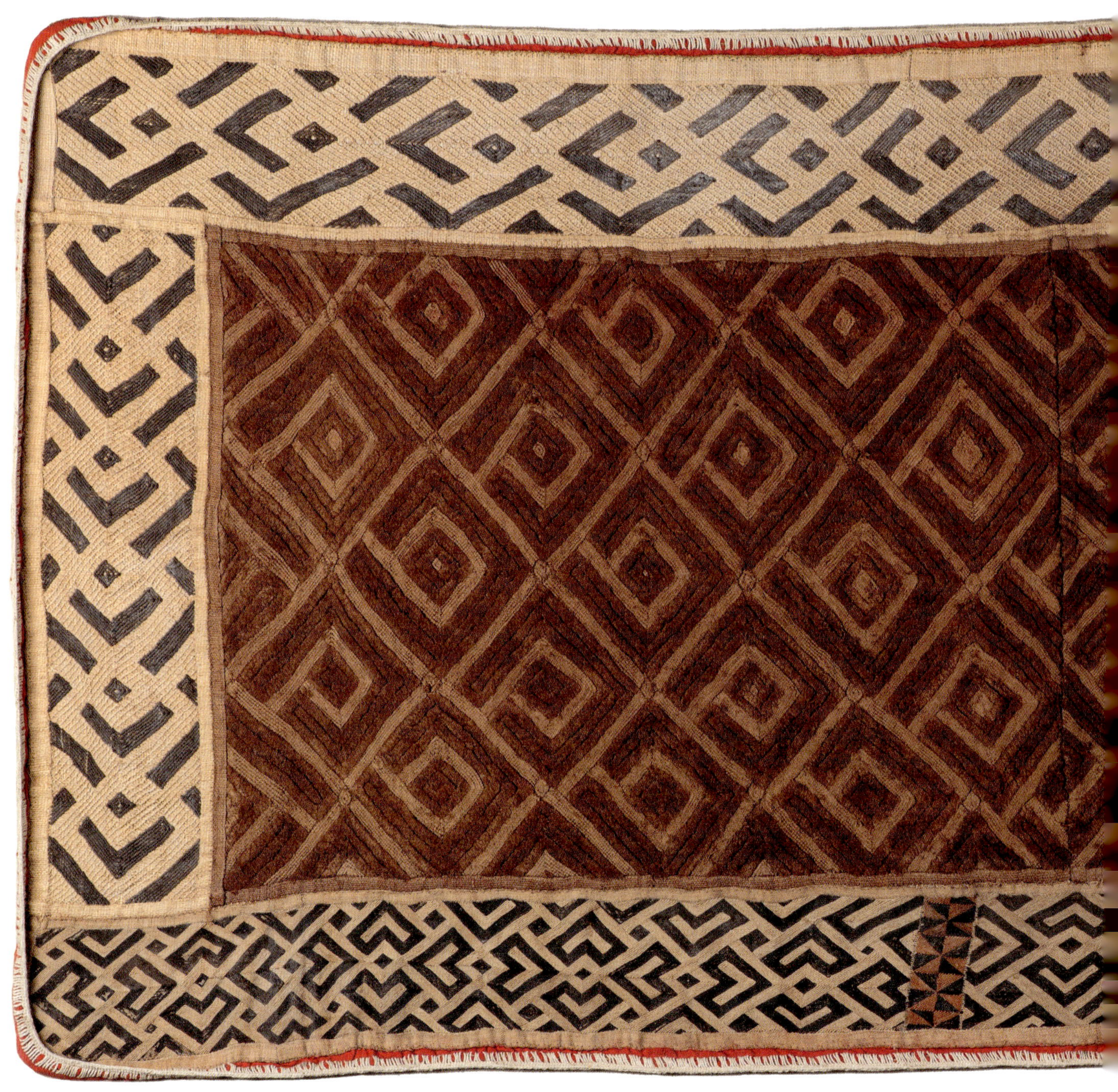

Cat. 36
Woman's dance or funerary overskirt, Kuba
People (Bushong Group), D R Congo, Kasai region,
20th century. Raffia palm fiber, natural redwood
bark colorant, synthetic indigo dyes; stem stitch
and cut-pile embroidery, 73⅝ × 35⅛ × 1¼ inches
(187 × 89.2 × 3.2 cm) (framed). 2020.24.49

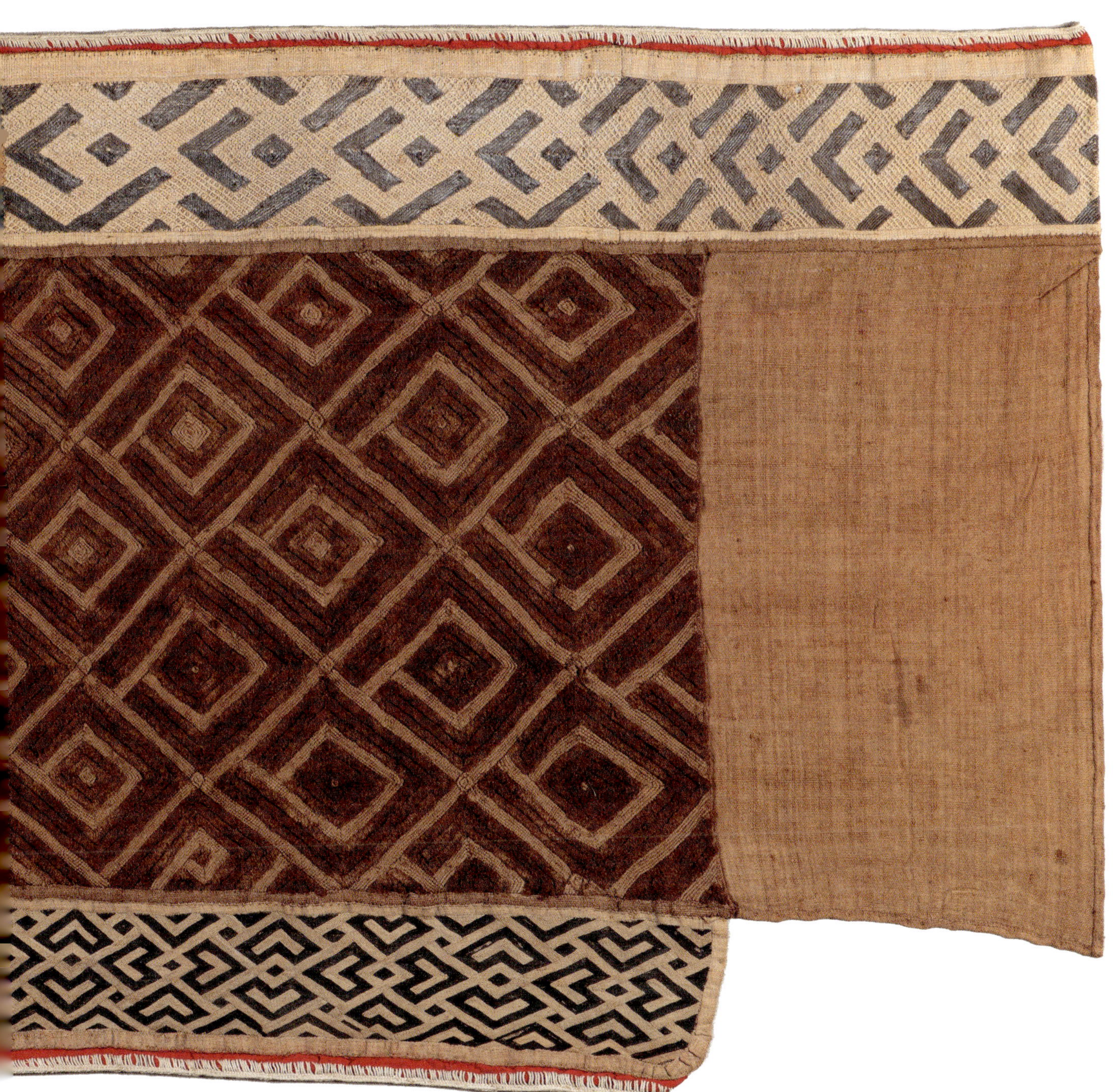

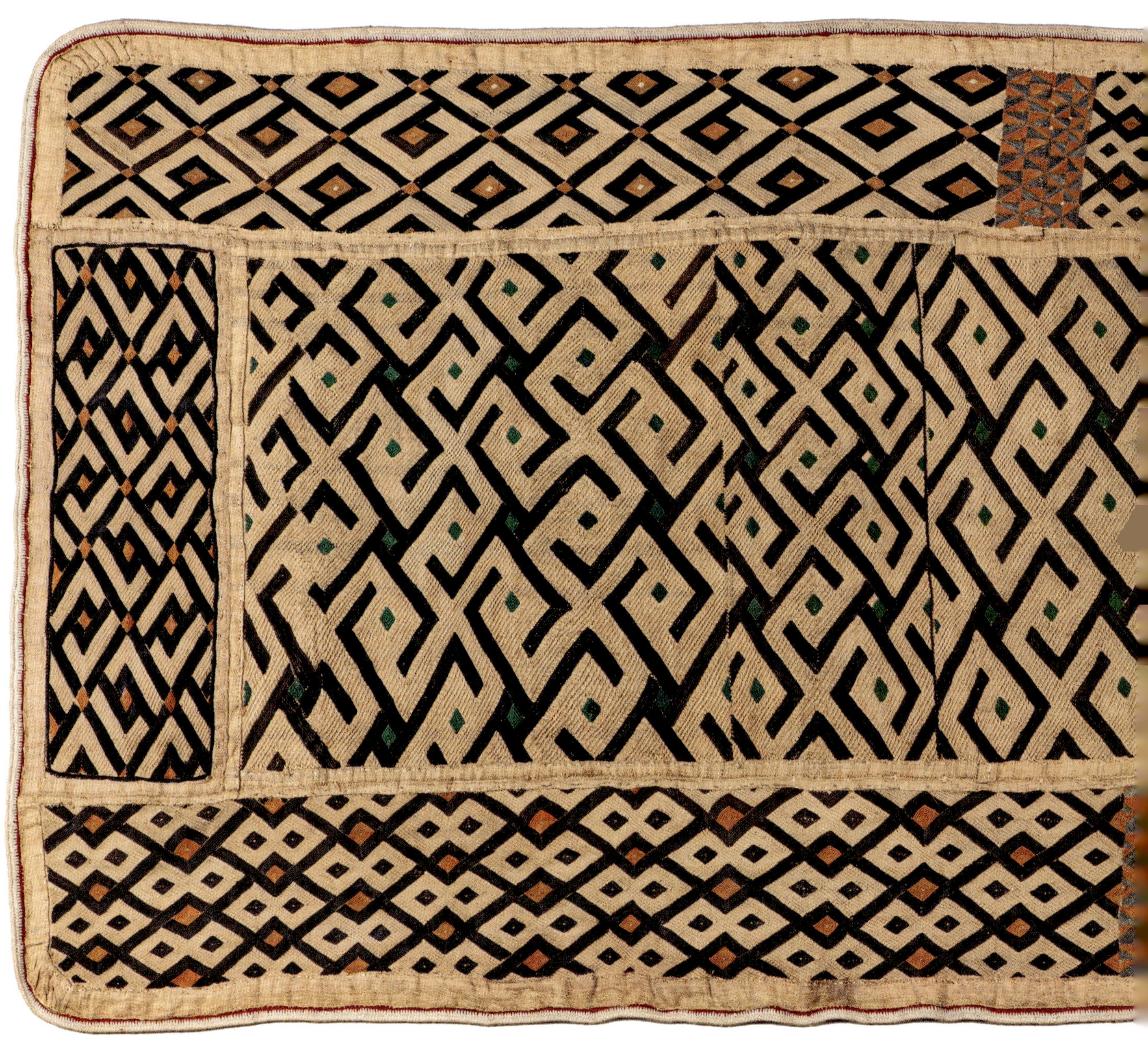

Cat. 37
Woman's dance overskirt, Kuba People (Bushong Group), D R Congo, Kasai region, 20th century. Raffia palm fiber, natural and synthetic dyes; stem stitch embroidery, 74¾ × 35⅛ × 1¼ inches (189.9 × 89.2 × 3.2 cm) (framed). 2020.24.48

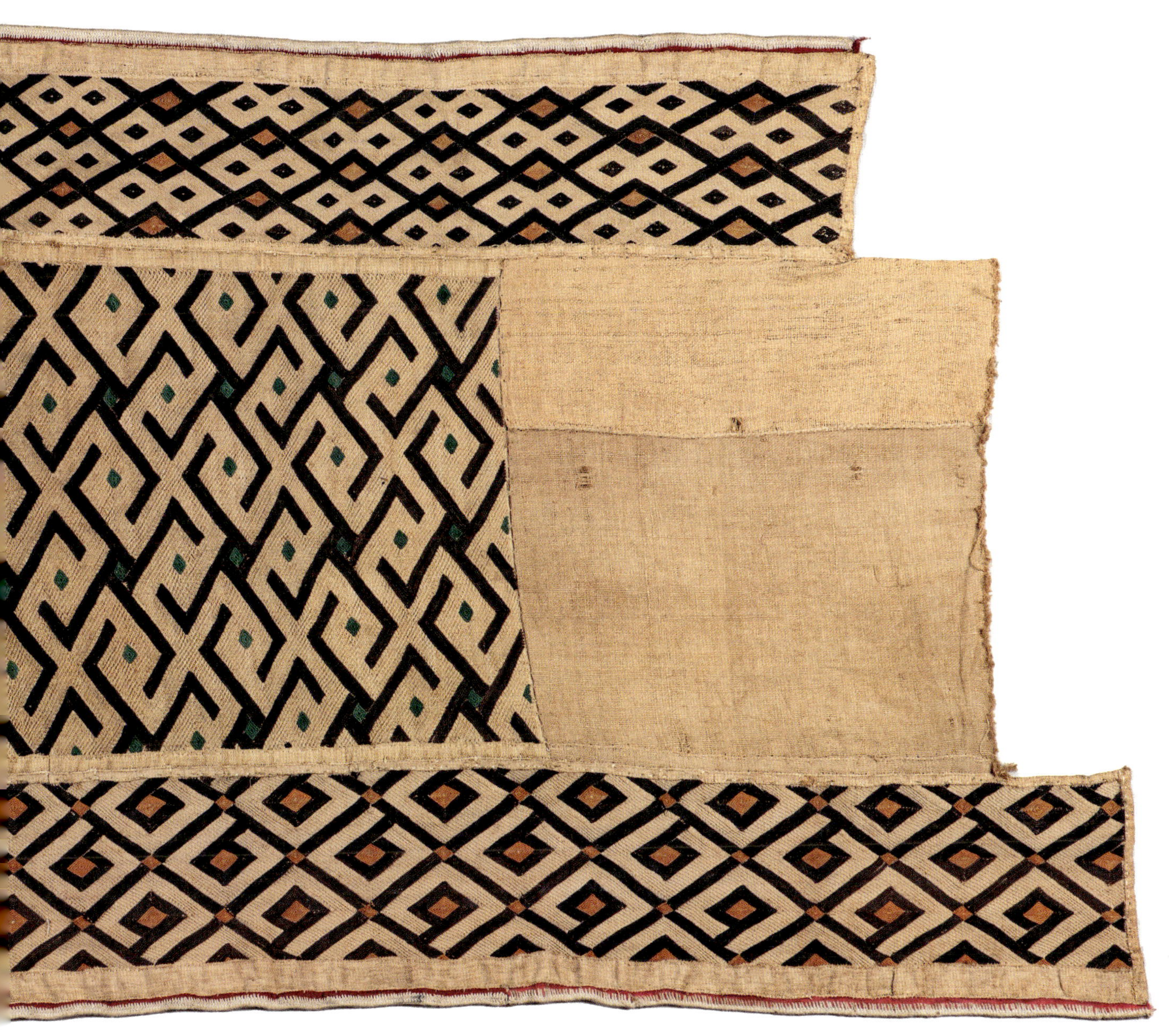

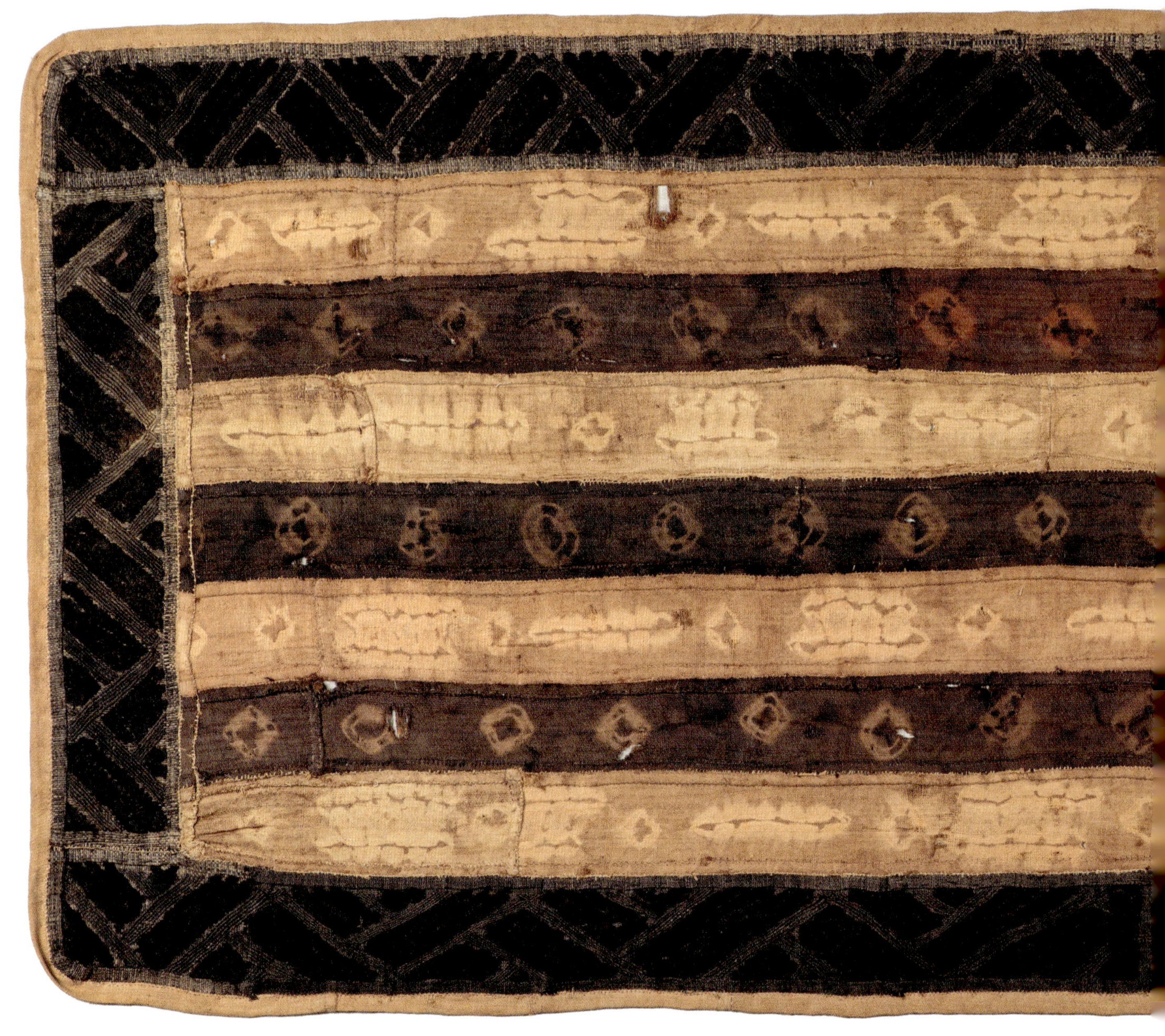

Cat. 38
Woman's dance overskirt, Kuba People (probably
Bushong Group), D R Congo, Kasai region,
20th century. Raffia palm fiber, natural dyes;
stem stitch and cut-pile embroidery (borders);
tie dye (center field), 75 × 33⅝ × 1¼ inches
(190.5 × 85.4 × 3.2 cm) (framed). 2020.24.46

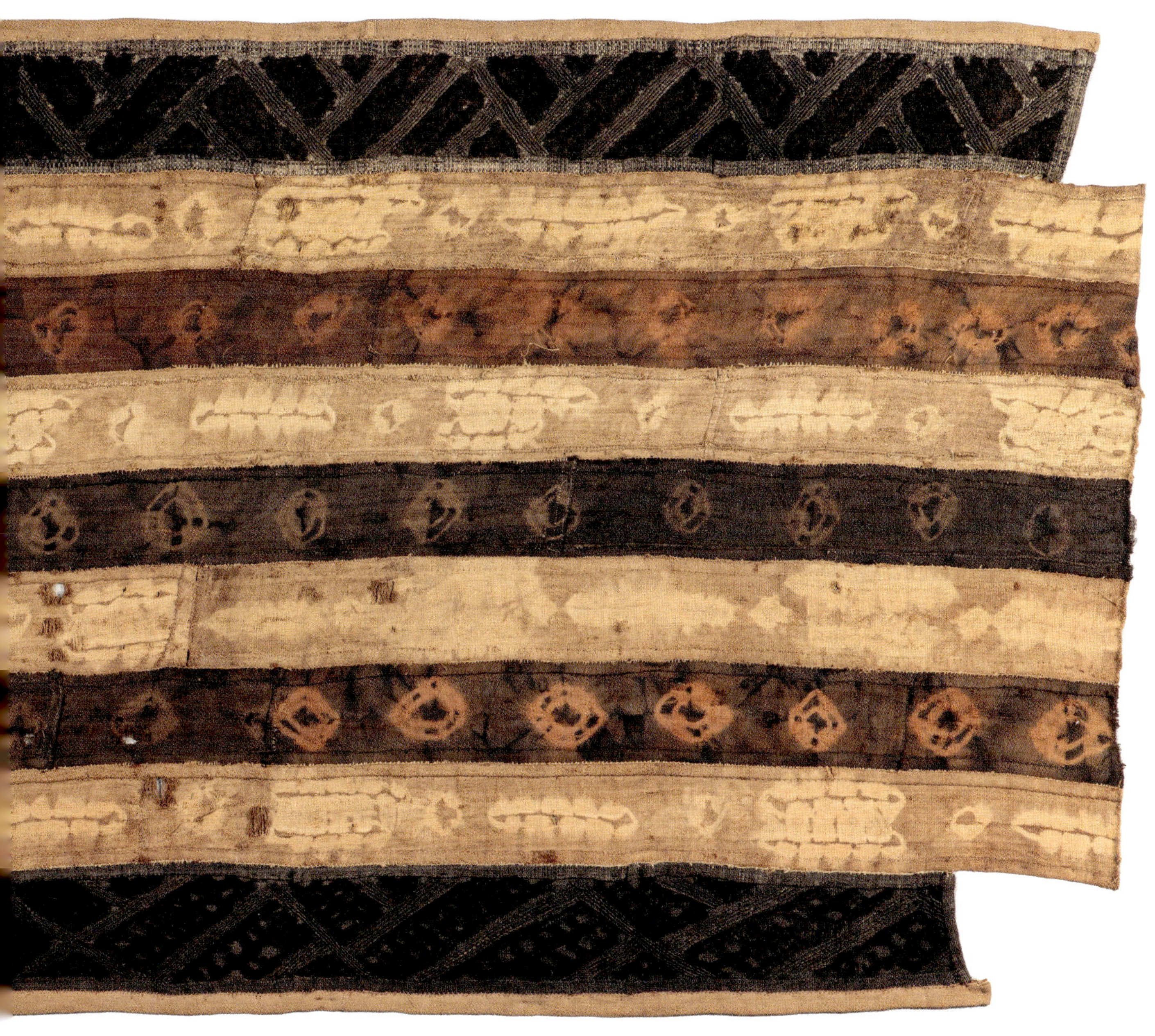

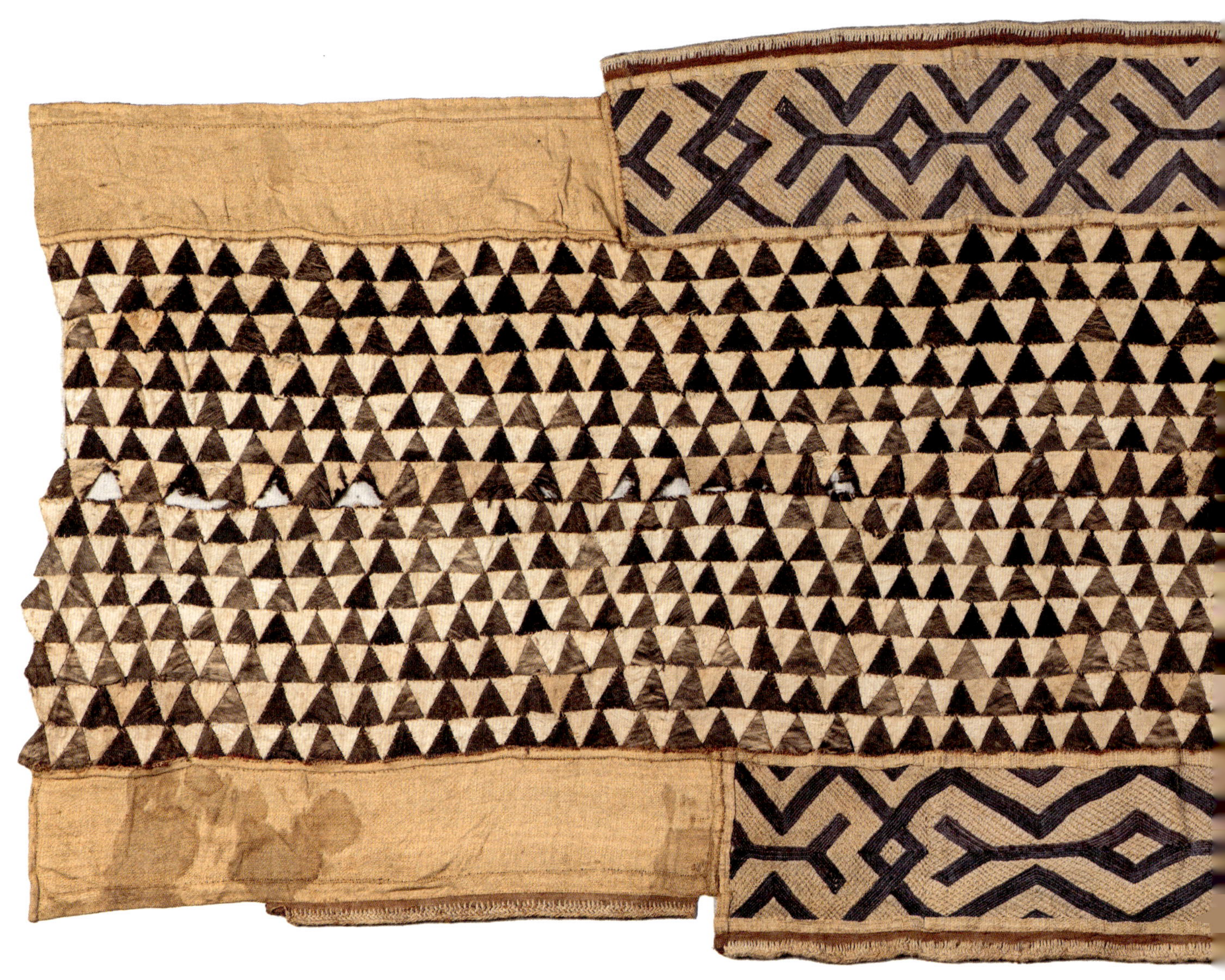

Cat. 39
Woman's dance overskirt, Kuba People
(Bushong Group), D R Congo, Kasai region,
20th century. Raffia palm fiber; stem stitch
embroidery (borders); piece dyed and lightened
bark cloth (center field), 87⅜ × 36⅛ × 1¼ inches
(221.9 × 91.8 × 3.2 cm) (framed). 2020.24.47

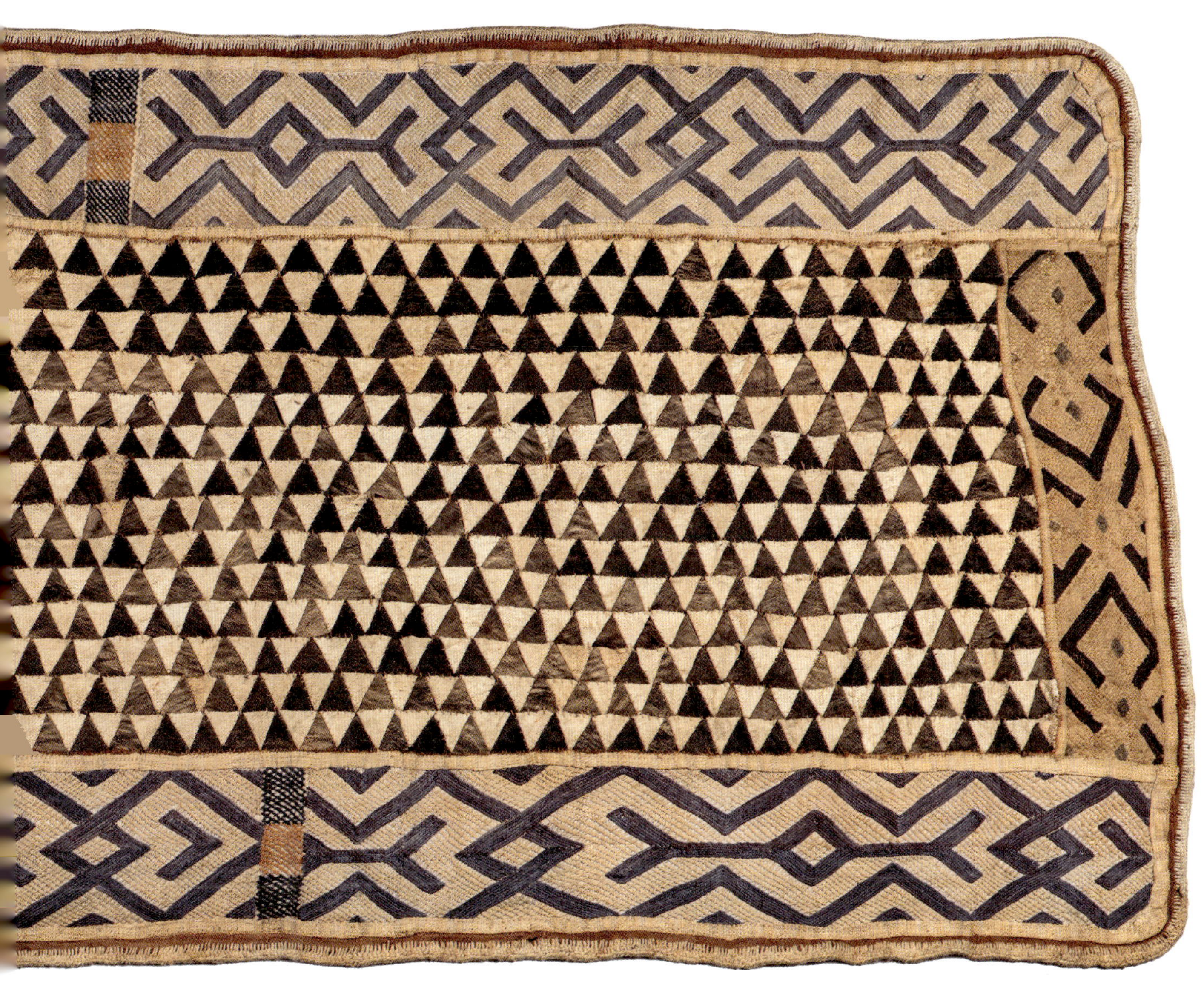

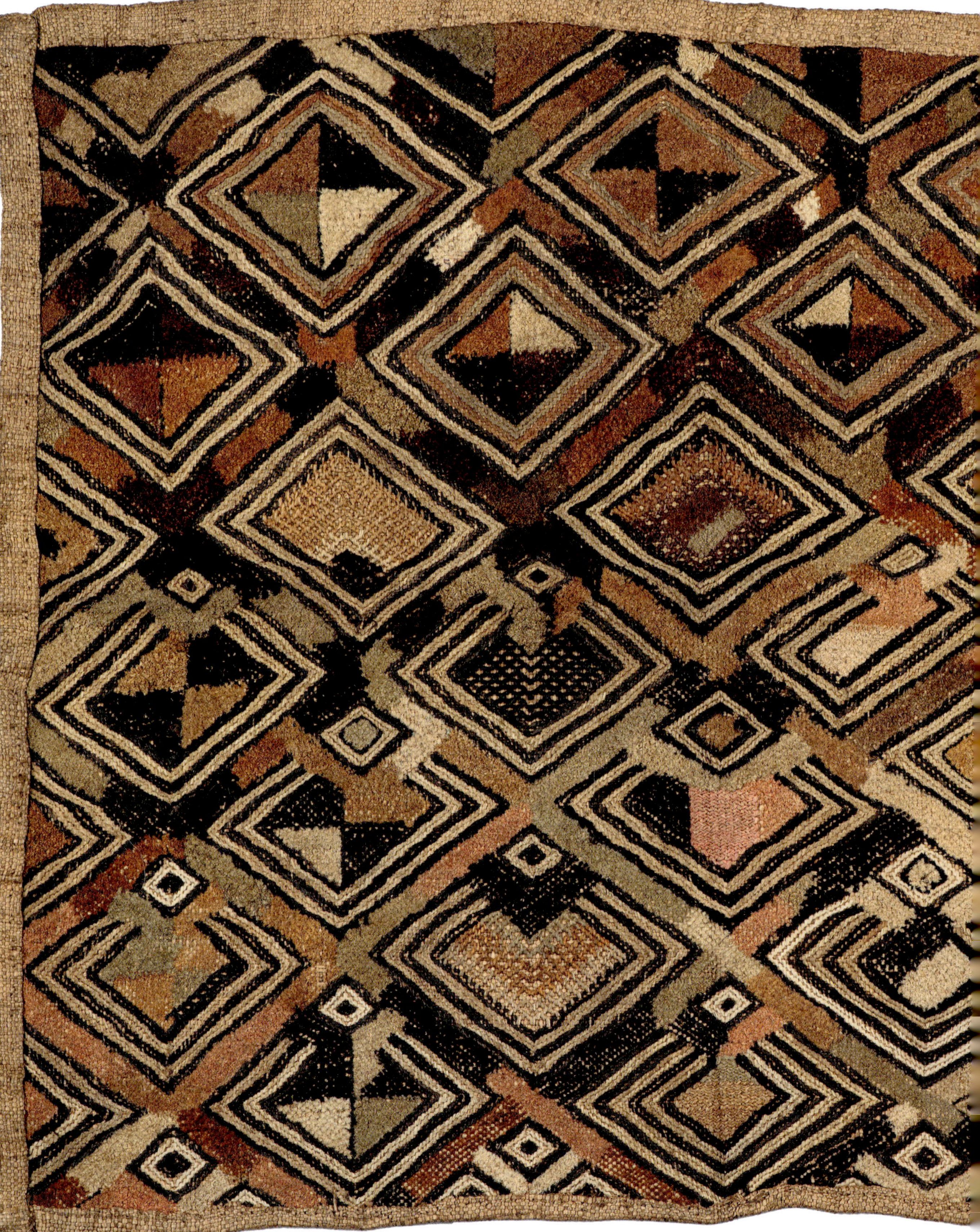

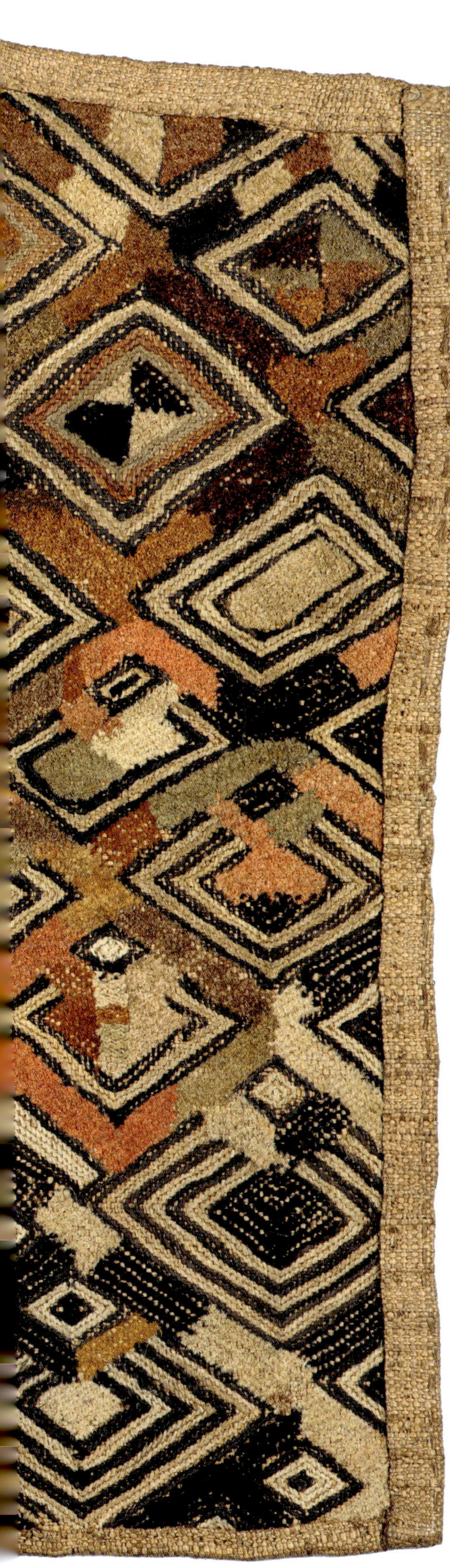

Cat. 40
Prestige Panel, 20⅛ × 17 inches
(51.1 × 43.2 cm). 2020.24.38

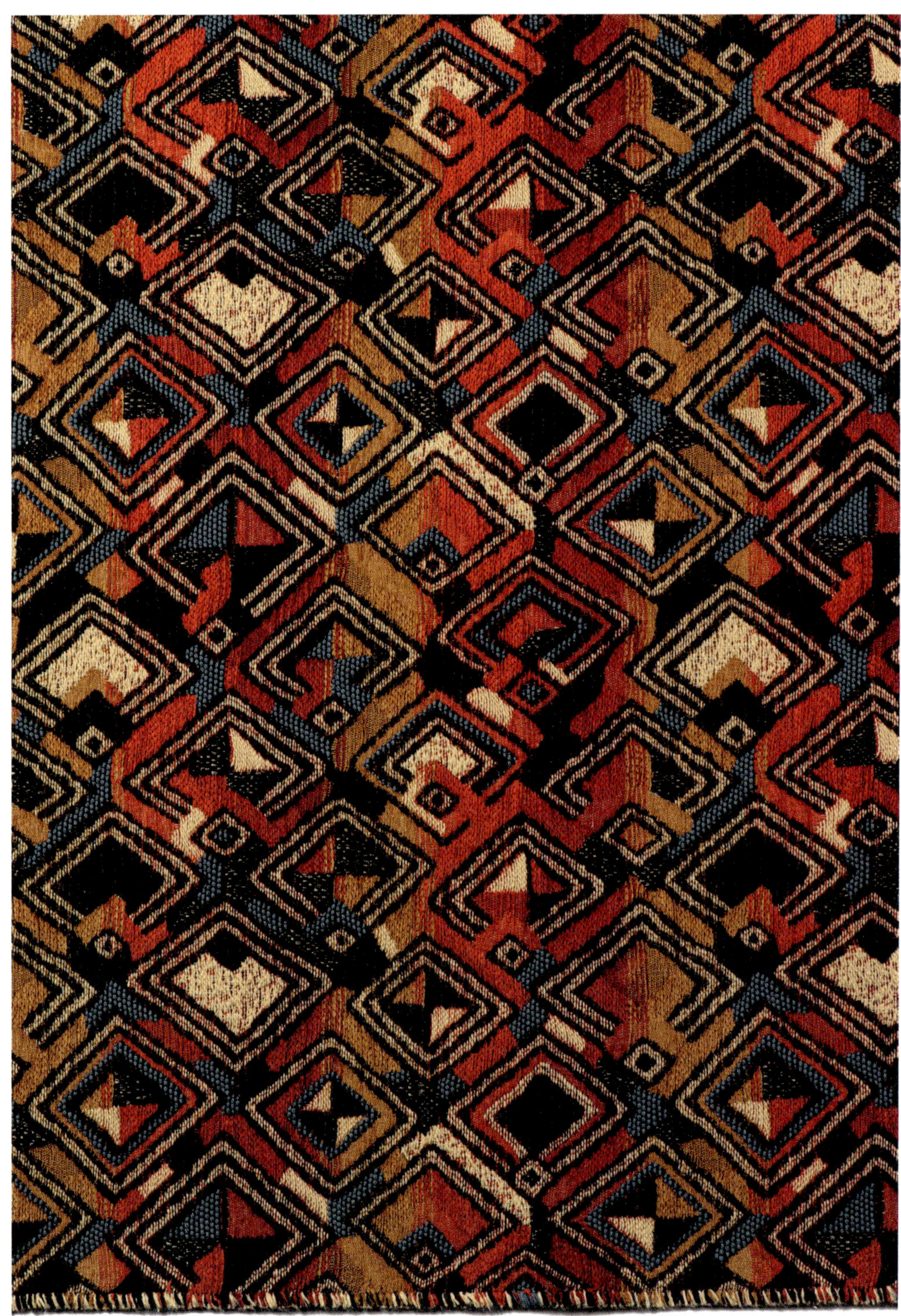

Cat. 41
Wesley Mancini (designer; American, b. 1952);
Valdese Weavers (manufacturer; United States,
1915–), *Oprisa* furnishing fabric, 2023. Fiber blend,
jacquard weave, 55¾ inches (141.6 cm) wide.
Gift of Valdese Weavers. 2024.19.5

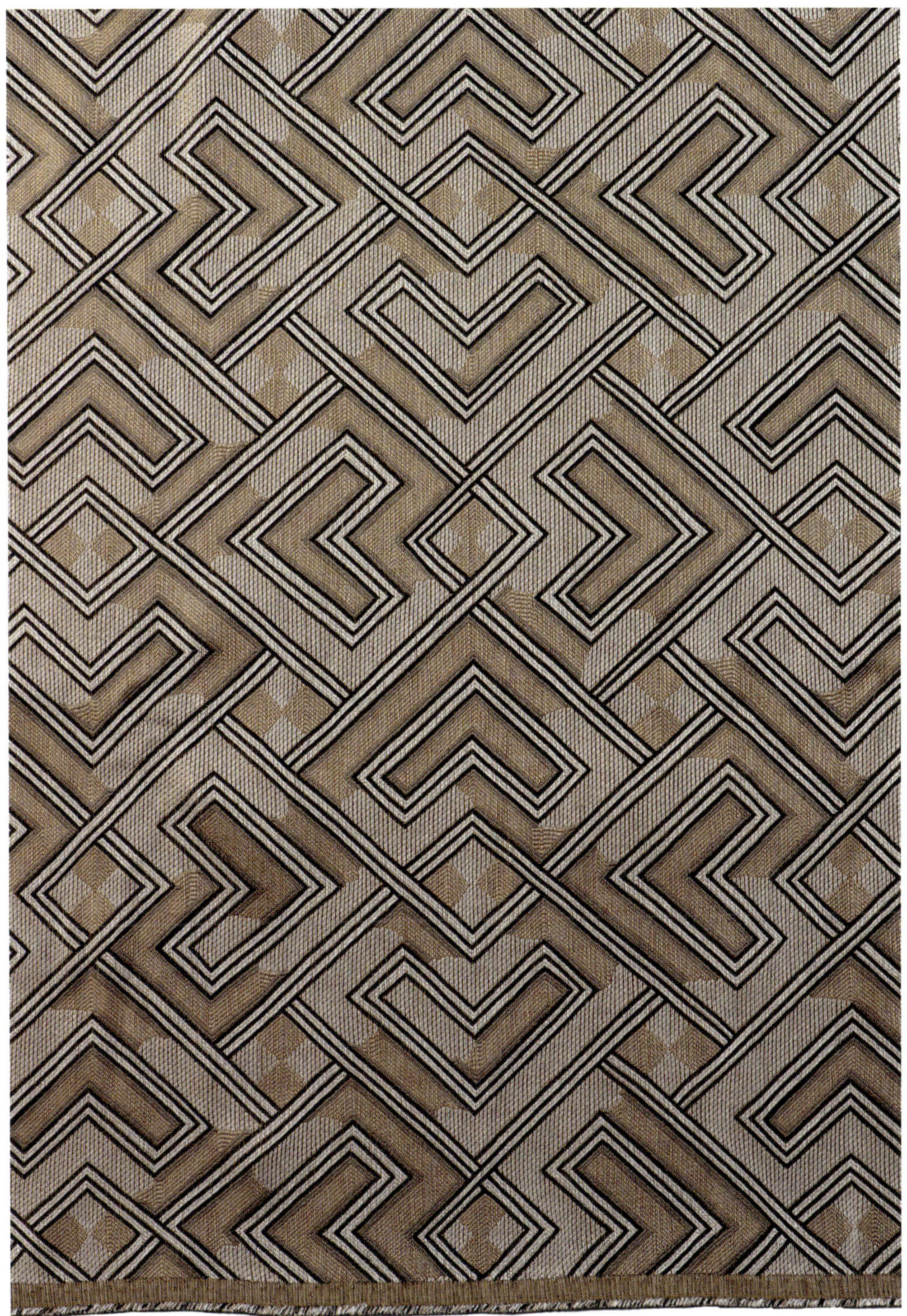

Cat. 42
Wesley Mancini (designer; American, b. 1952); Nardes,
LLC (manufacturer; Turkey, 2010–); Villa (textile mill;
Bursa, Turkey); Untitled, 2023. Furnishing fabric,
viscose and polyester, jacquard weave, 144 inches
(365.8 cm) long. Gift of Wesley Mancini. 2024.19.1

Cat. 43
Wesley Mancini (designer; American, b. 1952);
Valdese Weavers (manufacturer; United States,
1915–), *Birshon* furnishing fabric, 2023. Fiber
blend, jacquard weave, 55½ inches (141 cm) wide.
Gift of Valdese Weavers. 2024.19.4

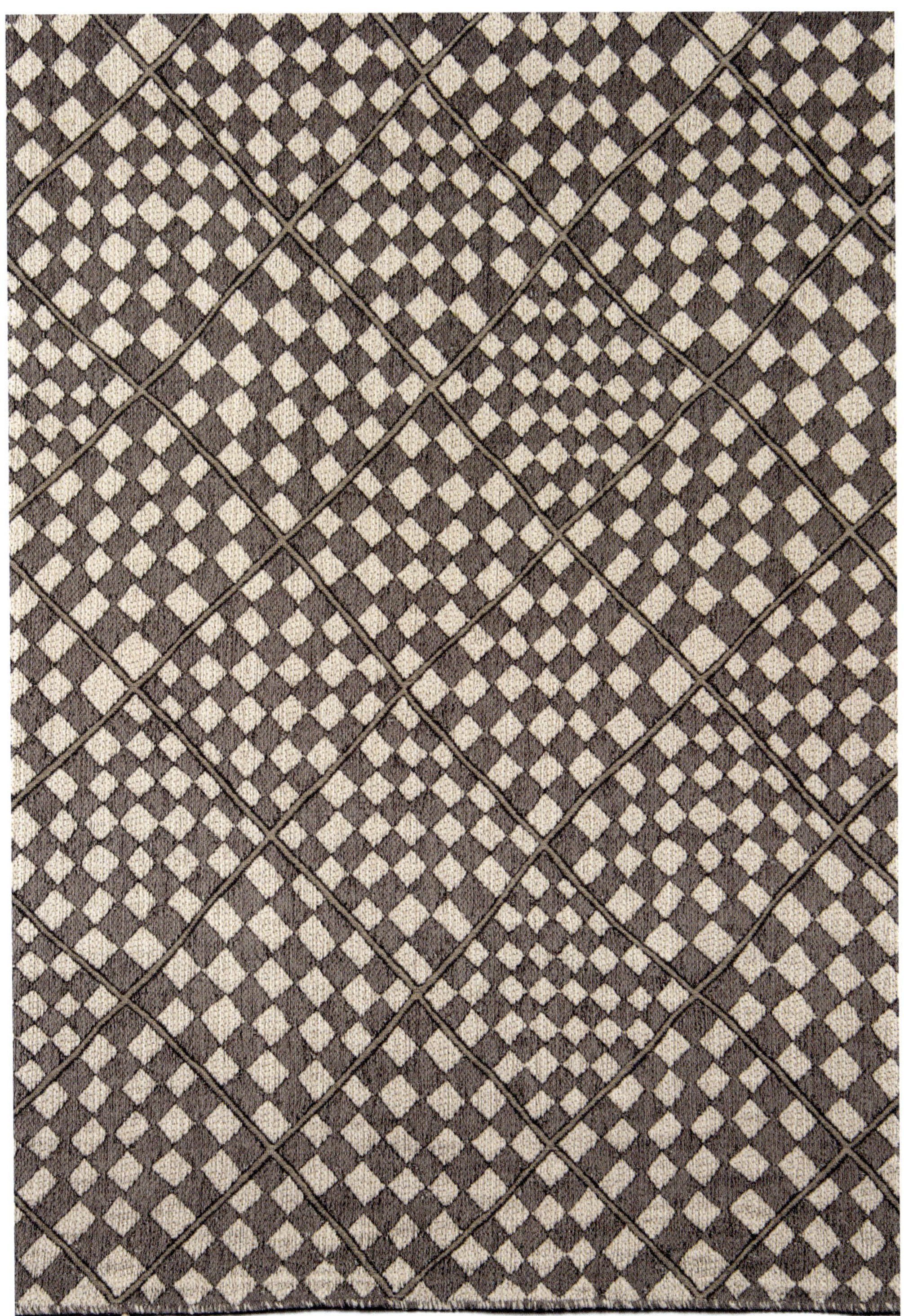

Cat. 44
Wesley Mancini (designer; American, b. 1952);
Valdese Weavers (manufacturer; United States,
1915–), *Malana* furnishing fabric, 2023. Fiber blend,
jacquard weave, 55¾ inches (141.6 cm) wide.
Gift of Valdese Weavers. 2024.19.3

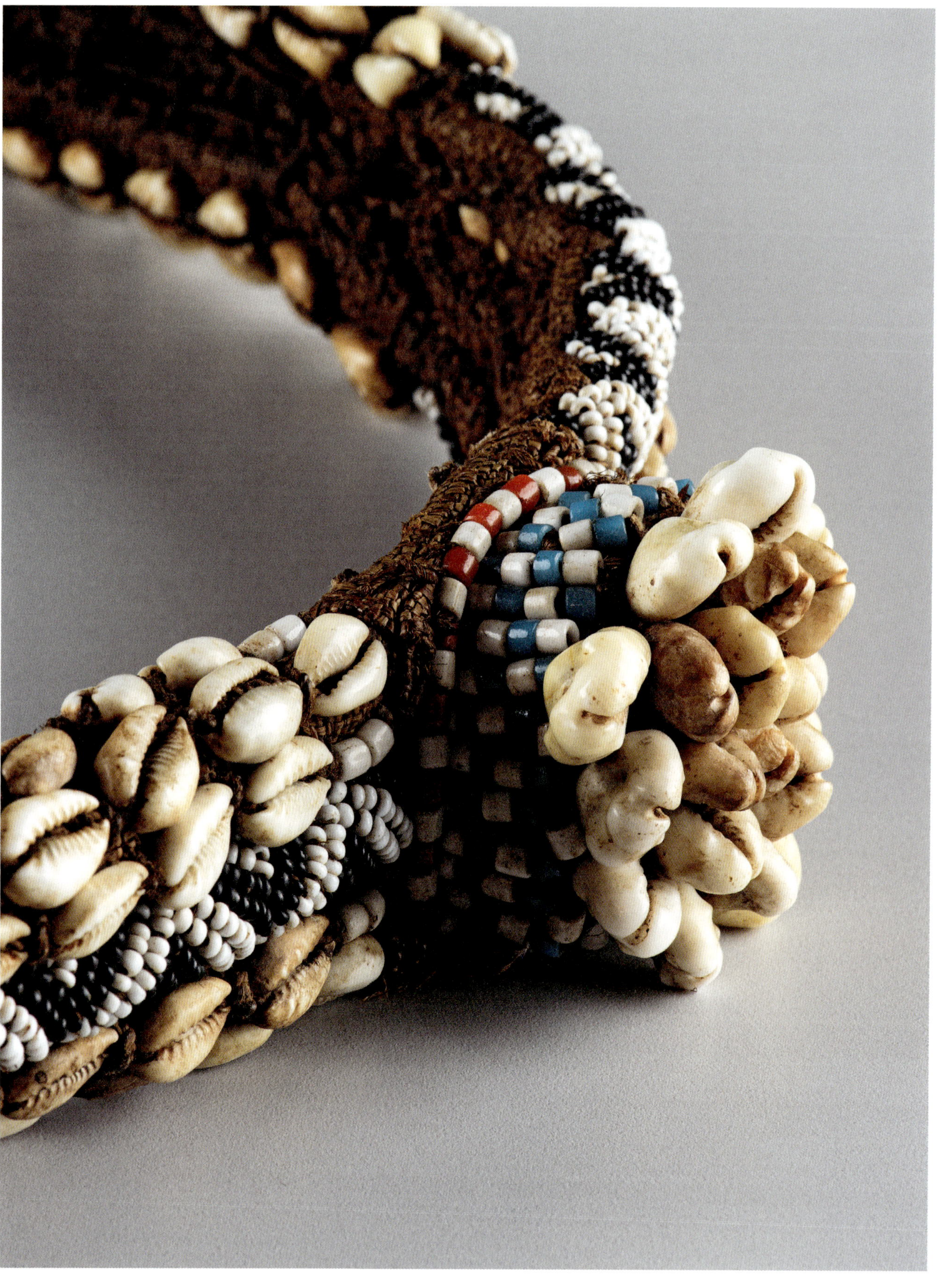

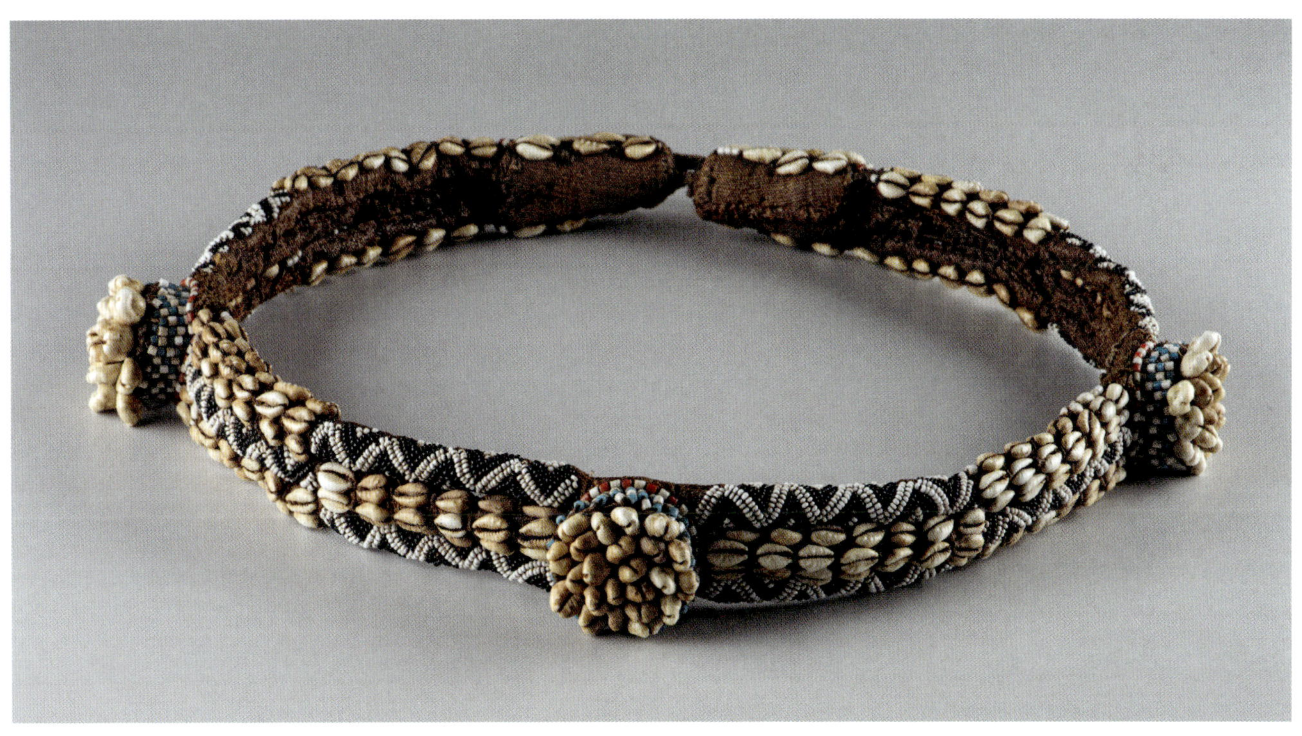

Cat. 45
Woman's ceremonial belt (Nkody Makwoom), Kuba
People (Bushong Group), D R Congo, Kasai region,
20th century. Raffia palm fiber, cowrie shells,
glass beads; plain weave, 2½ × 48¾ × 2⅛ inches
(6.4 × 123.8 × 5.4 cm). 2020.24.44

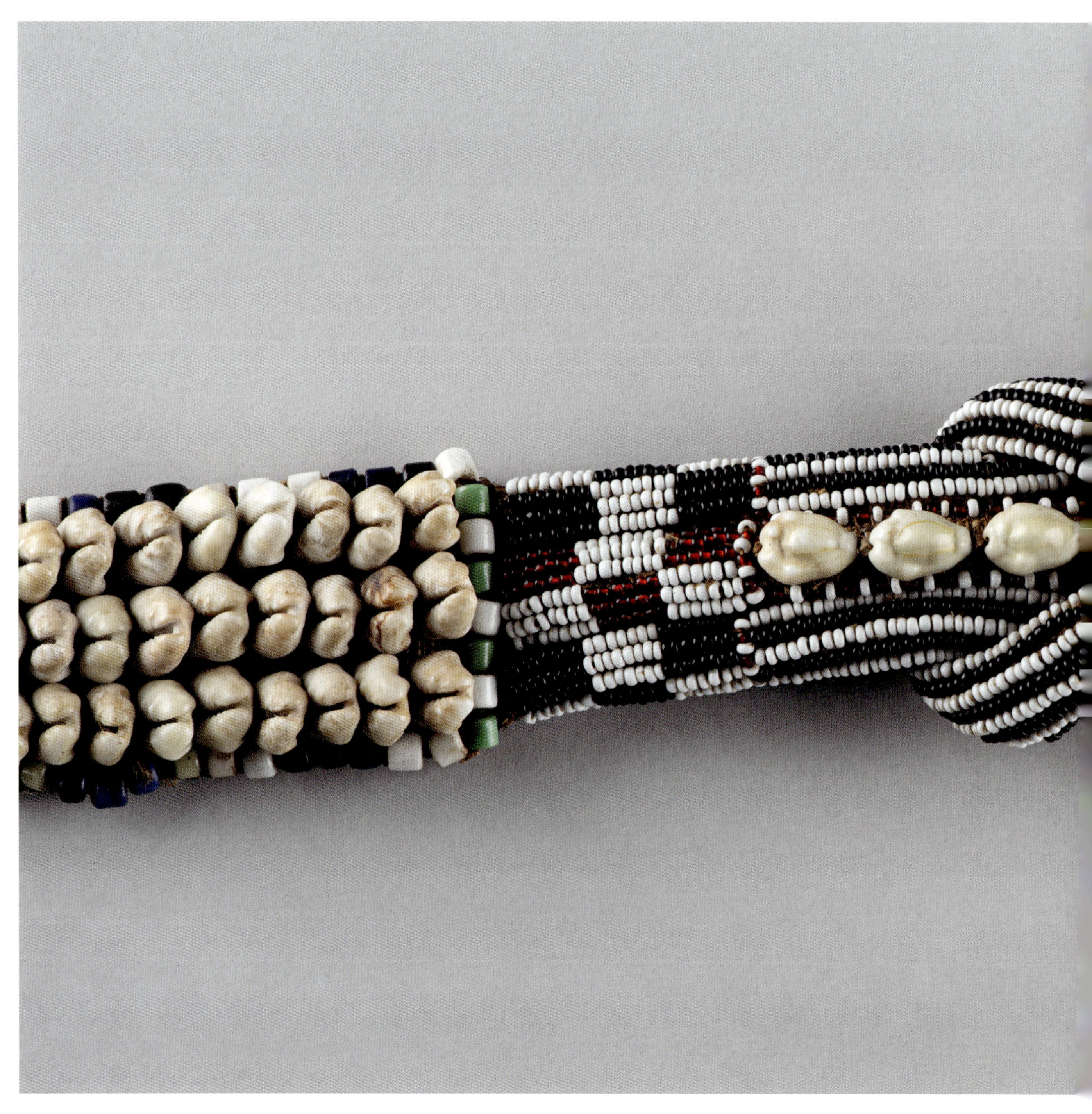

Cat. 46
Woman's ceremonial belt (Nkody Mu-Ikup)
(detail), Kuba People (Bushong Group), D R
Congo, Kasai region, 20th century. Raffia palm
fiber, cowrie shells, glass beads; plain weave,
2¼ × 45 × 1½ inches (5.7 × 114.3 × 3.8 cm).
2020.24.45

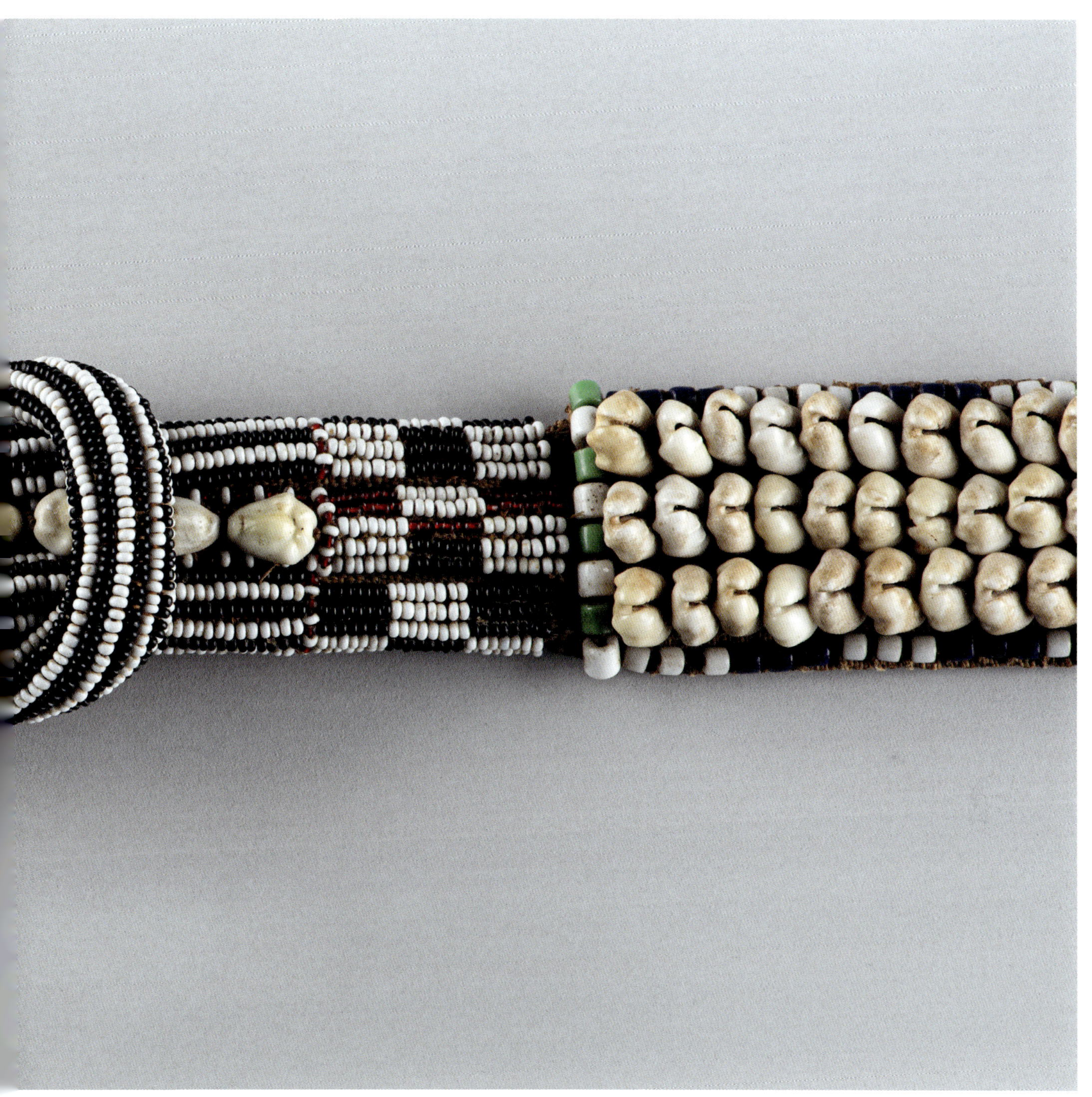

Notes

1   Hilary Spurling et al., *Matisse, His Art and His Textiles: The Fabric of Dreams*, exh. cat. (London: Royal Academy of Arts, 2004), 32.

2   "Primitive Negro Art, Chiefly From the Belgian Congo," Brooklyn Museum, April 11–May 20, 1923: https://www.brooklynmuseum.org/opencollection/exhibitions/698.

3   In light of Lesley Lokko's propositions—as the first woman of African descent to curate the Venice Architecture Biennale (18th edition), with the title "Africa: Laboratory of the Future"—it is time we repositioned the African continent and its diaspora as the starting point for conversations about the future.

4   This is a reference to the term "majority world," introduced by Bangladeshi photographer and activist Shahidul Alam as a direct critique of the Western world hegemony, highlighting the fact that "North America constitutes 5 percent of the world's population and Europe is about twice that."

5   Alisa La Gamma with Christine Giuntini, "Out of Kongo and into the Kunsthammer," in A. La Gamma, *Kongo: Power and Majesty* (New York: The Metropolitan Museum of Art, 2015), 22, 133–58.

6   Patricia Darish, "'A Land of Great Promise.' Exploration and Kuba-Decorated Textiles in the Late Nineteenth Century," in *Kuba Textiles: Geometry in Form, Space, and Time*, ed. Marie-Thérèse Brincard (Purchase, NY: Neuberger Museum of Art, 2015), 23–28.

7   Ibid.

8   Notable exhibition catalogues that cite Kuba textiles as artistic sources include *Matisse, His Art and His Textiles* (2004), *Au royaume du signe* (1988), and *Beyond Bloomsbury: Designs of the Omega Workshops 1913–19* (2009). See Selected Bibliography, pp. 92–93.

9   Alain Locke, "Note on African Art. 1924," in *Primitivism and Twentieth-Century Art: A Documentary History*, ed. Jack Flam (Berkeley: University of California Press, 2003), 191.

10 Gerstein, *Beyond Bloomsbury*, 93.

11 Roger Fry, "Negro Art," in R. Fry, *Last Lectures* (Cambridge: The University Press, 1939), 80, quoted by Gerstein, ibid.

12 Roger Fry, "Sensibility," in ibid., 24–35. Also quoted by Gerstein, ibid.

13 This textile can be accessed online: https://www.britishmuseum.org/collection/object/E_Af1909-0513-406.

14 Carl E. Schorske, "Foreword," in Jane Kallir, *Viennese Design and the Wiener Werkstätte* (New York: George Braziller, 1986), 8–9.

15 Verena Traeger, "Gustav Klimt and African Art: Kuba Affinities," in *Kuba Textiles*, ed. Brincard, 71–72.

16 Ibid.

17 Angela Völker, *Textiles of the Wiener Werkstätte 1910–1932* (New York: Thames and Hudson, 1994), 10.

18 The Werkstätte archive is available to view online at the MAK – Museum of Applied Arts, Vienna.

19 See a 1940 textile design by Richard Riemerschmid (a German architect affiliated with the Viennese Secession) in the Print Department, Museum of Modern Art, New York, and also a 1905 furnishing fabric (no. 185.1985.14), as well as a design by Stölzl (no. 407.1988). See other Kuba-related designs by Stölzl at www.guntastolzl.org and by Preiswerk at The Metropolitan Museum of Art, New York (inv. no. 484089).

20 The abundant Kuba-like imagery scattered throughout French design of the period includes carpets photographed by Thérèse Bonney, such as "Penetration" by Joubert and Petit for Décoration Intérieure Moderne (D.I.M) (1925) and "Rug in Geometric Design" by Max Vibert for Studium-Louvre (1925); Dutch designer C.A. Lion Cachet's mohair cushion (1925); decorative patterns for fabric and paper such as those by René Gabriel published in *Les Echos des industries d'art* (1927), Sonia Delaunay in *Tapis et tissus* (1929), E.A. Séguy in *Prismes* (1933), André Garcelon in *Inspirations : 80 Motifs en couleur* (1930), and Edouard Benedictus in *Nouvelles variations* (n.d.); as well as fabrics by Chanel, Chantal, Agnès, and Bianchini-Férier.

21 Alastair Duncan, *Art Deco Complete: The Definitive Guide to the Decorative Arts of the 1920s and 1930s* (New York: Abrams, 2009), 7.

22 Jacques Damase, *Sonia Delaunay: Fashion and Fabrics* (New York: Abrams, 1991), 128, 170; Jacques Damase, *Sonia Delaunay : Rythmes et couleurs* (Paris: Hermann, 1971), 221. One version of this design printed in brown and black actually renders a Kuba-like color scheme (now in the collection of the Musée des Tissus et des Arts Décoratifs, Lyon).

23 Sherry Buckberrough, "Delaunay Design: Aesthetics, Immigration, and the New Woman," *Art Journal* 54, no. 1 (Spring 1995): 53–55.

24 Henri Clouzot, *Tissus nègres* (Paris: Librairie des Arts Décoratifs, 1931), n.p.; translation by the present author.

25 Wendy A. Grossman, *Man Ray, African Art, and the Modernist Lens* (Washington, DC: International Arts and Artists, 2009), 138–39.

26 Alain Locke, "Legacy of the Ancestral Arts. 1925," in *Primitivism and Twentieth-Century Art*, ed. Flam, 201.

27 See Elizabeth Catlett, *Roots* (1981); Loïs Mailou Jones, *Ode to Kinshasa* (1972); James A. Porter, *Dismounted Spirit* (1959).

28 See *Guitar and Pipe (Polka)* (1920–21), Philadelphia Museum of Art; *Vase, Palette, and Mandolin* (1936), San Francisco Museum of Modern Art; *Vase, Palette, and Skull* (1939), The Kreeger Museum, Washington, DC.

29 See *Red Interior, Still Life on a Blue Table* (1947), Kunstsammlung Nordrhein-Westfalen, Düsseldorf, and *The Dream* (1940), private collection, published in Spurling et al., *Matisse, His Art and His Textiles*, 138.

30 Grossman, *Man Ray*, 138–39; Spurling et al., *Matisse, His Art and His Textiles*, 31–32.

31 John Mack, "Making and Seeing: Matisse and the Understanding of Kuba Pattern," *Journal of Art Historiography*, no. 7 (December 2012): 4–7.

32 Susan Hannel, "'Africana' Textiles: Imitation, Adaptation, and Transformation during the Jazz Age," *Textile: The Journal of Cloth and Culture* 4, no. 1 (Spring 2006): 70, 77–85; Buckberrough, "Delaunay Design," 51.

33 Unpublished papers and materials in the Delaunay archives possibly contain information to the contrary, but to date the present author has not seen any statement by the artist referring to Kuba textiles.

34 Damase, *Rythmes et couleurs*, 219, 222.

35 In "The Influence of Painting on Fashion Design" (1926), Delaunay stated: "If there are geometric forms, it is because these simple and manageable elements have appeared suitable for the distribution of colors whose relations constitute the real object of our search, but these geometric forms do not characterize our art." In *The New Art of Color: The Writings of Robert and Sonia Delaunay*, ed. Arthur A. Cohen (New York: The Viking Press, 1978), 207.

36 Hannel, "'Africana' Textiles," 71, 74.

37 Ibid., 78–85.

38 Margaret Breuning, "Primitive Negro Art on Exhibition," *New York Post*, April 14, 1923. Accessed online at Culin Archival Collection, Brooklyn Museum of Art.

39 Wendy A. Grossman, "*Mode au Congo*: Travails of the Traveling Hats," 2022, accessed at https://www.metmuseum.org/perspectives/articles/2022/9/mode-au-congo/.

40 Ibid.

41 Grossman, *Man Ray*, 48.

42 There are 42 variants of the artist's name based on signatures he, or others, affixed to his works. Vincent Meessen, "Recapturing the Fable of Modernity," in *Tshela Tendu and Vincent Meessen: Patterns For (Re)cognition,* exh. cat. (Brussels: Centre for Fine Arts/Snoeck Publishers, 2017), 29.

43 Florian Knothe and Estela Ibáñez-García, eds., *Colours of Congo: Patterns, Symbols and Narratives in 20th-Century Congolese Paintings*, exh. cat. (Hong Kong: University Museum and Art Gallery, 2021), 69; Thomas Bayet, "Origins of Congolese Painting," in ibid., 39–41.

44 Meessen, "Recapturing the Fable," 27.

45 *Tshela Tendu and Vincent Meessen*, 45.

46 Patricia Darish, "'This is Our Wealth': Towards an Understanding of a Kuba Textile Aesthetic," in *Elvehjem Museum of Art Bulletin* (Madison: University of Wisconsin, 1996), 66.

47 David Revere McFadden, *Jack Lenor Larsen: Creator and Collector* (London: Merrell, 2004), 140–41.

48 See Patrick Kelly's ensemble in the Philadelphia Museum of Art (Accession number 329525) and Alphadi's dress in the Victoria and Albert Museum, London (Accession number T.60:1to2-2022).

Selected Bibliography

Breuning, Margaret. "Primitive Negro Art on Exhibition." *New York Post*, April 14, 1923. Accessed online at Culin Archival Collection, Brooklyn Museum of Art.

Buckberrough, Sherry. "Delaunay Design: Aesthetics, Immigration, and the New Woman," *Art Journal* 54, no. 1 (Spring 1995): 51–55.

Clouzot, Henri. *Tissus nègres*. Paris: Librairie des Arts Décoratifs, 1931.

Cohen, Arthur A., ed. *The New Art of Color: The Writings of Robert and Sonia Delaunay*. New York: The Viking Press, 1978.

Damase, Jacques. *Sonia Delaunay: Fashion and Fabrics*. New York: Abrams, 1991.

———. *Sonia Delaunay : Rythmes et couleurs*. Paris: Hermann, 1971.

Darish, Patricia. "'A Land of Great Promise.' Exploration and Kuba-Decorated Textiles in the Late Nineteenth Century." In *Kuba Textiles: Geometry in Form, Space, and Time*, ed. Marie-Thérèse Brincard. Purchase, NY: Neuberger Museum of Art, 2015.

———. "'This is Our Wealth': Towards an Understanding of a Kuba Textile Aesthetic." In *Elvehjem Museum of Art Bulletin*. Madison: University of Wisconsin, 1996.

Delaunay, Sonia. *Ses Peintures, ses objets, ses tissus simultanés, ses modes*. Paris: Librairie des Arts Décoratifs, 1925.

———. *Tapis et tissus*. Paris: Moreau, 1929.

Dorogova, Waleria, and Katia Baudin, eds. *Maison Sonia Delaunay*. Krefeld: Hatje Cantz, 2022.

Duncan, Alastair. *Art Deco Complete: The Definitive Guide to the Decorative Arts of the 1920s and 1930s*. New York: Abrams, 2009.

Falgayrettes, Christiane, and John Mack, Georges Meurant, Margrit Rowell et al. *Au royaume du signe, appliqués sur toile des Kuba.* Paris: Musée Dapper/ Éditions Adam Biro, 1988.

Fry, Roger. *Last Lectures*. Cambridge: The University Press, 1939.

Gerstein, Alexandra. *Beyond Bloomsbury: Designs of the Omega Workshops 1913–19*. Exh. cat. London: The Courtauld Gallery, 2009.

Godefroy, Cécile. *Sonia Delaunay : Sa mode, ses tableaux, ses tissus*. Paris: Flammarion, 2004.

Grossman, Wendy A. *Man Ray, African Art, and the Modernist Lens*. Washington, DC: International Arts and Artists, 2009.

———. *"Mode au Congo*: Travails of the Traveling Hats." Accessed online at The Metropolitan Museum of Art: https://www.metmuseum.org/perspectives/ articles/2022/9/mode-au-congo/.

Hannel, Susan. "'Africana' Textiles: Imitation, Adaptation, and Transformation during the Jazz Age." *Textile: The Journal of Cloth and Culture* 4, no. 1 (Spring 2006): 68–103.

Kallir, Jane. *Viennese Design and the Wiener Werkstätte*. New York: George Braziller, 1986.

Knothe, Florian, and Estela Ibáñez-García, eds. *Colours of Congo: Patterns, Symbols and Narratives in 20th-Century Congolese Paintings*. Exh. cat. Hong Kong: University Museum and Art Gallery, 2021.

La Gamma, Alisa. *Kongo: Power and Majesty*. New York: The Metropolitan Museum of Art, 2015.

Locke, Alain. "Legacy of the Ancestral Arts. 1925." In *Primitivism and Twentieth-Century Art: A Documentary History*, ed. Jack Flam. Berkeley: University of California Press, 2003.

———. "Note on African Art. 1924." In ibid.

Mack, John. "Making and Seeing: Matisse and the Understanding of Kuba Pattern." *Journal of Art Historiography*, no. 7 (December 2012): 1–19.

Malochet, Annette, and Matteo Bianchi. *Sonia Delaunay. Atelier Simultané 1923–1934*. Milan: Skira, 2006.

McFadden, David Revere. *Jack Lenor Larsen: Creator and Collector*. London: Merrell, 2004.

McQuaid, Matilda, and Susan Brown, eds. *Color Moves: Art & Fashion by Sonia Delaunay*. Exh. cat. New York: Smithsonian Cooper-Hewitt, National Design Museum, 2011.

Moraga, Vanessa Drake. *Weaving Abstraction: Kuba Textiles and the Woven Art of Central Africa*. Washington, DC: The Textile Museum, 2011.

Spurling, Hilary, et al., *Matisse, His Art and His Textiles: The Fabric of Dreams.* Exh. cat. London: Royal Academy of Arts, 2004.

Traeger, Verena. "Gustav Klimt and African Art: Kuba Affinities." In *Kuba Textiles: Geometry in Form, Space, and Time*, ed. Marie-Thérèse Brincard. Purchase, NY: Neuberger Museum of Art, 2015.

Troy, Virginia Gardner. *The Modernist Textile: Europe and America 1890–1940*. Aldershot, UK: Lund Humphries, 2006.

Tshela Tendu and Vincent Meessen: Patterns For (Re)cognition. Exh. cat. Brussels: Centre for Fine Arts/Snoeck Publishers, 2017.

Völker, Angela. *Textiles of the Wiener Werkstätte 1910–1932*. New York: Thames and Hudson, 1994.

OTHER WORKS CONSULTED

Childs, Adrienne L. *Riffs and Relations: African American Artists and the European Modernist Tradition*. Exh. cat. Washington, DC: The Phillips Collection, 2019.

Damase, Jacques. *Sonia Delaunay : Notes biographiques rédigées par Edouard Mustelier*. Paris: Galerie de Varenne, 1971.

Leymarie, Jean, Achille Bonito Oliva, and Annette Malochet. *Sonia Delaunay. Atelier Simultané 1923–1934*. Exh. cat. Venice: Galleria Bevilacqua La Masa, 2002.

Since the Harlem Renaissance: 50 Years of Afro-American Art. Exh. cat. Lewisburg, PA: The Center Gallery of Bucknell University, 1985.

Sonia Delaunay. Exh. cat. London: Tate Publishing, 2015.

Acknowledgments

The delight in composing these words of gratitude is in great part because *Designing Dynamism* was delayed, allowing more time for deeper research and connections with a larger group of individuals, resulting in a better exhibition and book. *Designing Dynamism: Kuba Textiles from the D R Congo, The Wesley Mancini Collection* celebrates the unique design aesthetic of a particular type of African embroidery, long esteemed by curators and scholars but hardly known in the greater art and design world. So, I am thankful that Wesley Mancini, himself a textile designer, recognized the genius of Kuba patterns and techniques years ago, and decided to collect the best he could find. Mancini's gift of 52 prestige squares is enhanced by additional Kuba women's overskirts and belts. Collectively, they fill a gap in the Mint's holdings of both textile design and African art, and provide an abundance of cultural discovery for our community.

There were many twists and turns in the development of this project, and at every juncture there was support from Todd A. Herman, President & CEO, Jennifer Sudul Edwards, Chief Curator and Curator of Contemporary Art, and Michele Leopold, Senior Director of Collections & Exhibitions. *Designing Dynamism* is an ambitious undertaking and Meghann Zekan, Chief Exhibition Designer, Che Machado, Chief Preparator, and Eric Speer, Associate Registrar, handled the challenges with patience and esprit de corps. Rebecca O'Malley, Exhibition Coordinator, kept us and the schedule moving forward; she has my gratitude for the necessary nudges. Sara Renaud, Visual Resources Coordinator, Scott Waltz, Senior Preparator, Derek Rosenberry and Jylik Buissereth, Preparators, and Shelby McVicker, Environmental and Exhibition Graphic Designer, assisted with a myriad of details.

I am grateful to the Advancement team for their crucial role in securing funding for *Designing Dynamism*. Hillary Cooper, Chief Advancement Officer, Amy Tribble, Director of Corporate Relations and Advancement Operations, and Martha Snell, Grants Manager, explored new strategies and new sponsorship opportunities with astounding success.

Slow looking at the prestige textiles with Joel Smeltzer, Head of School and Gallery Programs, resulted in the artful renderings in this book and exhibition. I am grateful to Cynthia Moreno, Senior Director of Learning and Engagement, for her commitment to programming that broadens our knowledge of African design, and to Maggie Kapitan, Public Programs Educator, who handled local and international arrangements. Jennifer Winford, Associate Librarian, assisted with research, adding more books on African design, textiles, and Kuba culture to the Mint's collection, as well as securing titles via interlibrary loan.

Much appreciation to Jennifer Williams, Director of Accounting, Hannah Snyder, Director of Retail Operations, Clayton Sealey, Senior Director of Marketing and Communications, and the entire M & C team for their talent and ongoing enthusiasm for *Designing Dynamism*.

Since 1990, I have been extremely lucky to have seen and studied great Kuba textiles in the US and Europe, from appliqué skirts, caps and headgear to prestige cloths. I learned a lot from collectors and scholars. Working on *Designing Dynamism* provided the opportunity to expand my understanding of the materiality of Kuba textiles through extensive sessions with several leading textile conservators. Patricia Ewer, Principal of Textile Objects Conservation LLC, who has consulted on many Mint textile and fashion projects, carried out a preliminary survey of the Mint's Kuba textiles and indulged my many questions. I benefited from conversations about Kuba dyestuffs, chemistry, and raffia with Christine Giuntini, Textile Conservator, The Metropolitan Museum of Art's Michael C. Rockefeller Wing. Howard Sutcliffe, Principal, River Region Costume and Textile Conservation, cleaned and treated every prestige square in the exhibition, and provided a solution to their installation. Collaborating with him continues to be educational and fun.

Sadly, the individual makers of these prestige textiles are unknown to us, so the installation and book are focused on the vibrant and pulsating patterns, the motifs and textures, and the important cultural narrative, past, present, and future. Given the focus on the design elements, it was critical to find an architect/designer who could imagine spectacular ways of organizing the gallery spaces. Stephen Burks, Principal of Stephen Burks Man Made, immediately came to mind, since his blending of the handmade and the industrial in his furniture and product designs, his reverence for makers (particularly textile artists, in the US, Philippines, Cambodia, and Africa, giving them agency), and his incessant advocating for a new design and production paradigm, are unmatched. Along with Malika Leiper, Cultural Director, Stephen Burks Man Made, he created an environment that takes the visitor on an emotional journey from colonial history to Kuba futurism, bringing to life the curatorial vision for *Designing Dynamism*. Stephen Burks's newfound passion for Kuba textiles, and his perspective on their relevancy today, are expressed in his poignant essay included in this catalogue.

The main catalogue text was written by Vanessa Drake Moraga. A preeminent scholar of Andean and African textiles, her work on Kuba textiles contains much intellectual rigor, sensitivity, and insight. Her exhaustive research on Kuba patterns and modernism has resulted in a text that is both factual and revelatory, a sampling of her vast knowledge of the subject. I am grateful to her for her insistence on getting it right, going above and beyond to elevate her fine text with the perfect images.

The stunning plate-section images in this book are the work of Brandon Scott, contract photographer, once again displaying his talent for object photography.

Colleagues who assisted with my research include Dr. Christine Checinska, Senior Curator, African and Diaspora Textiles and Fashion, V & A South Kensington; Dr. Vanessa Thaxton-Ward, Director, Hampton University Museum; Rainald Franz, Curator of Ceramics and Glass, and Provenance Research Officer, MAK – Museum of Applied Arts, Vienna; Matilda McQuaid, Acting Director of Curatorial, Cooper Hewitt, Smithsonian Design Museum; and Martina D'Amato and Titi Halle, Cora Ginsburg, LLC.

Making books with D Giles Limited is a pleasure, and I must thank Dan Giles for asking me to add more to this exhibition catalogue—more text, more images—when my inclination was to do the opposite. Since collaborating on several exhibition catalogues together, the team at Giles—Allison McCormick, Louise Ramsay, Liz Japes, Jenny Wilson, and Ocky Murray—and I have an intuitive way of working, and I am thankful to them for our respectful collaborations. Editing is superbly handled, and the striking design of this book is a testament to D Giles Limited's ongoing aesthetic achievements.

Designing Dynamism, in its conception, evolution, and implementation, has required much time and effort. While it is a cliché to say "oh, but it's a labor of love," what is true is that the extra adrenaline and stamina come from those who support Craft, Design & Fashion full stop. Among them, the amazing individuals who comprise the Mint Museum of Craft, Design & Fashion Collections Council, led by Jill Walker Kelly, Chair, have sustained me with their encouragement, friendship, and keen interest in this project.

Most of all, my deepest gratitude goes to team Craft, Design & Fashion. Our tiny but mighty team is adept at multitasking, pivoting, and remaining solution-oriented. Bridget Kerr, Fashion Fellow, took on departmental tasks when I could not, cheerfully and thoroughly. Rebecca E. Elliot, Associate Curator of Craft, Design & Fashion, whose technological and copy-editing skills far outweigh mine, played a significant role at every stage of the manuscript preparation. Participating in many aspects of *Designing Dynamism*, Rebecca enhanced this project with her curiosity and suggestions; she has my profound thanks.

I can't thank Jay Everette, National Director of Community Relations, Philanthropy and Community Impact, Wells Fargo Public Affairs, enough for his interest and trust.

This book is dedicated to Daniel Hugo Fruman.

Annie Carlano
Senior Curator, Craft, Design & Fashion

This book was published to coincide with the exhibition,
*Designing Dynamism: Kuba Textiles from the D R Congo,
The Wesley Mancini Collection*, organized by The Mint Museum,
Charlotte, North Carolina, February 21–August 24, 2026

Mint Museum Randolph
2730 Randolph Road
Charlotte, North Carolina 28207
www.mintmuseum.org

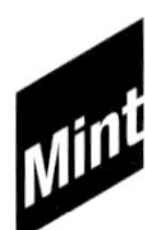

First published in 2026 by GILES
An imprint of D Giles Limited
66 High Street,
Lewes, BN7 1XG, UK
https://gilesltd.com

ISBN (hardcover): 978-1-913875-89-3

Designing Dynamism is presented with generous support
from Wells Fargo.

The Mint Museum is supported, in part, by the Infusion Fund and its
generous donors; the North Carolina Arts Council, a division of the
Department of Cultural Resources; the City of Charlotte; and its members.

Library of Congress Cataloging-in-Publication Data

Names: Carlano, Annie, editor. | Moraga, Vanessa Drake, author. | Burks,
Stephen, 1969- author. | Herman, Todd A., writer of foreword. |
Smeltzer, Joel, illustrator. | Mint Museum (Charlotte, N.C.)

Title: Designing dynamism : Kuba textiles from the D R Congo, the Wesley
Mancini collection / Annie Carlano, editor ; Vanessa Drake Moraga,
Stephen Burks, Todd A. Herman ; illustrations by Joel Smeltzer ; the
Mint Museum in association with D Giles Limited.

Description: Charlotte : The Mint Museum, 2026. | Includes bibliographical
references.

Identifiers: LCCN 2025019459 | ISBN 9781913875893 (hardcover)

Subjects: LCSH: Art, Kuba--Exhibitions. | Textile crafts--Congo (Democratic
Republic)--Exhibitions. | Kuba (African people)--Exhibitions. | LCGFT:
Exhibition catalogs.

Classification: LCC N7399.C6 D47 2026 | DDC
746.089/96396--dc23/eng/20250619

LC record available at https://lccn.loc.gov/2025019459

Copy-edited and proof-read by Jenny Wilson
Designed by Ocky Murray
Produced by GILES, an imprint of D Giles Limited
Printed and bound in Italy

All measurements are in inches and centimeters

Front and back cover: Detail of Cat. 10

Frontispiece: Cat. 1 Prestige Panel (detail), 27 × 25⅛ × 1¼ inches
(68.6 × 63.8 × 3.2 cm) (framed). 2020.24.8

Page 4: Detail of Cat. 13

Page 6: Cat. 2 Prestige Panel (detail), 20½ × 16¾ inches
(52 × 42.5 cm). 2020.24.40

Page 18: Detail of Cat. 27

Pages 42–43: Detail of Cat. 34

Image Credits

Full captions for Prestige Panels unless otherwise indicated:

Cats. 1, 2, 5, 6, 8: Prestige Panel (detail), Kuba People (Shoowa Group),
D R Congo, Kasai region, ca. 1980. Raffia palm fiber, natural dyes;
stem stitch and cut-pile embroidery. Collection of The Mint Museum.
The Wesley Mancini Textile Collection.

Cats. 10–30, 32–35, 40: Prestige Panel, Kuba People (Shoowa Group),
D R Congo, Kasai region, ca. 1980. Raffia palm fiber, natural dyes;
stem stitch and cut-pile embroidery. Collection of The Mint Museum.
The Wesley Mancini Textile Collection.

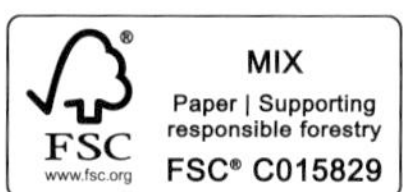